11-28-64

\$ 3.50

1964-65

D1500348

THE DYNAMICS OF FORGIVENESS

by James G. Emerson, Jr.

Here, in a book as creative as the implication of its title, is a study that provides vital redefinitions in Christian thinking. Its assumption is that there is a relationship between contemporary insights in theology and modern discoveries about the nature of personality. From this perspective it studies the place of forgiveness in the areas of parish life, personal health, and theological thought. Written from the context of parish experience and fostered by a program of parish research, the book tries to see what this " description from parish life " says about the church's changing views of forgiveness.

Dr. Emerson poses three major questions. The first is, Is there a correlation between the experience of forgiveness as a part of one's life and the description of personality as integrated and whole? He defines *realized forgiveness* in Pauline terms as " the freedom to be a new creature and a new creator." He shows evidence that the contextual nature of the church is that of the forgiveness which modern man seeks in psychiatry — and that integrity which Tillich calls " the courage to be."

The second question is, What is the correlation between the experience of forgiveness as understood in the history of the church and that experience which will be identified with the experience of forgiveness? He traces fully the development of the idea of forgiveness (in three aspects of context, instrument, and experience) through the Old and New Testaments and through the history of church thought, pointing out that all history, particularly all church history, might be written as the story of man's search to find forgiveness.

(Continued from front flap)

The third question asked is, Is there anything significant here for the whole matter of theological thought, Christian worship, and the work of the church? Dr. Emerson concludes that *realized forgiveness* is an experience which precedes and qualitatively changes all theological systems. Because this forgiveness is rooted in parish experience, parish theology must be reevaluated as the preface or vestibule of all theology — redefined as the bridge between the world of the church and the world of culture. It thus becomes the key to the problem of meeting the secularist and understanding why the church does not break through to him.

This is a book which makes a rich contribution to theological and pastoral thought. It speaks, too, to all Christians who strive for integrity and wholeness of being.

THE AUTHOR

James G. Emerson, Jr., was born in Palo Alto, California. After graduating from Stanford University, he continued his studies at Princeton Theological Seminary and the University of Chicago. At Princeton, Dr. Emerson served on the National Staff of the Interseminary Movement, was a traveling secretary for the S.V.M., and went to Europe in connection with the World Council. He has held charges in Pennsylvania, Illinois, and New York, is now pastor of the Westminster Presbyterian Church, Bloomfield, New Jersey, and Visiting Lecturer in Pastoral Theology at Princeton Theological Seminary.

Books by
JAMES G. EMERSON, JR.

Published by The Westminster Press ®

The Dynamics of Forgiveness
Divorce, the Church, and Remarriage

THE DYNAMICS
OF FORGIVENESS

by
James G. Emerson, Jr.

The Westminster Press

Philadelphia

PUBLISHED BY THE WESTMINSTER PRESS ®
PHILADELPHIA, PENNSYLVANIA 19107

PRINTED IN THE UNITED STATES OF AMERICA

*This book
is dedicated to my wife,
Margaret*

Contents

Acknowledgment

THIS book is the product of a parish and of theological study in the context of a parish. I am particularly indebted to the elders of the Westminster Presbyterian Church, Bloomfield, New Jersey, who committed themselves to pastoral research by establishing a program called the Westminster Institute of Pastoral Theology. The program involved a correlation of teaching, ministry, and research.

The initial work for this study was done in connection with a seminar of students at Bloomfield College. With that information as a base, three men from Princeton Seminary then spent a year with me in what proved to be the heart of the research experience. These men, William Craig, L. Blaine Libbey, and David Riddle, aided not only in the testing but also in the historical research. Miss Joan Malamud prepared the typed transcripts of many interview hours.

For assistance in the course of preparing the manuscript, I am indebted to Miss Helen Leithhauser of the Bloomfield College library, to Dr. Richard Gilbert and the facilities of the Center for Continuing Education at Princeton Seminary, and to the staff of the Princeton Theological Seminary library.

These chapters were first presented in lecture form at the Westminster Church. Mrs. Bronson Stout prepared the final manuscript, Mr. and Mrs. John Kreer read the manuscript, and my colleague, Rev. George M. Booker, and his wife served as copy and proof readers. To them, to the persons who allowed me to use material from my interviews with them, and to those who spent the time in taking the tests, I extend my thanks. Especially, however, I would mention my wife, to whom this book is affectionately dedicated, and our children and families. Margaret has not only checked the copy, but has also been a " sounding board " throughout the preparation of the material.

I am responsible for all the conclusions that are here, but, in truth, this is a book from the parish. It is written from observations of those to whom life has become meaningful when the relevancy of the Christian faith has been found.

J. G. E.

1

Why This Book Is Written

I INTRODUCTION

THIS book is both a protest and a confession. It is written by a pastor. More important, it is written from the context of parish experience. Most important is the fact that these experiences have been subjected to investigation by tested procedures. Out of this research comes a protest to theologians from a parish minister and to fellow pastors from a colleague.

This book is just a beginning. It attempts to give enough evidence to establish the place of forgiveness in theological thought, parish life, and personal health. I am not a church historian, a systematic theologian, or an authority on human behavior. From the perspective of the parish, however, I wish to raise questions for those who are experts in these disciplines; and I write in hopes of a response. Therefore, this book has a twofold purpose: to show the essential place of forgiveness in theological thought; to show the essential place of forgiveness in making the parish relevant.

II THE NATURE OF THE PROTEST

This protest is theological, pastoral, and personal.

Theologically, the protest is that theological thinking, for almost two thousand years, has not taken seriously the heart of the gospel. There have been noted exceptions. Yet most theologies have both recognized and ignored the center of the Scripture. The heart of the good news is the fact of forgiveness — not as a doctrine but as an experience. Intellectually, no theology that is genuinely Christian has ignored forgiveness as a doctrine. In some, it may have been a small segment of a chapter on the atonement. In others, like Ritschl's work, it may have been the overriding theme of the whole system. In view of the fact that Christ is to be called Jesus, "for he will save his people from their sins," this recognition could hardly be otherwise. Yet even Calvin, who observes the need to recover the place of forgiveness within the life of the church, missed dimensions of the implications of forgiveness in personal experience.

Historically, the failure to understand the dynamics of forgiveness has always had one of two results: reformation or heresy. The relation of Jesus to the Pharisees can be seen as an attempt at reform. In the sixteenth century, the sterility and mockery of confession and penance as used by Tetzel led to the need for recovering the experience of forgiveness. After having tried everything else, Luther led the Reformation. The Reformation produced different denominations in an effort to make forgiveness real in personal lives. In our own time, these very differences have resulted in a doctrinaire and culturally influenced church that is as inadequate at making forgiveness real as was the church prior to the sixteenth-century upheaval. Today, in what Clayton Morrison called the "unfinished reformation," there is the ecumenical movement. If ecumenicity becomes just a structural reorganization and fails to see its place in relation to forgiveness, the ecumenical movement will have failed and still another reformation will be needed.

Whenever the church has failed to take forgiveness seriously, if the result has not been reformation, it has been heresy. In the days of the early church, Tertullian was a great and concerned leader. Yet, toward the end of his life, he moved into Montanism. Why? Clearly, Tertullian was in search of something. In the first part of his life, he did much to help the church find a structure. His writings are full of suggestions for church procedure, ways of worship, and the actions of Christians. He made detailed suggestions about the steps people must take in order to experience the forgiveness of God. There is evidence to suggest that Tertullian moved into heresy in search of that which would make forgiveness real. The improvement of the structure of church government and procedure did not fulfill that search.

It is almost commonplace to point to the same phenomenon in the rise of Christian Science in nineteenth-century America. Religion in much of the nation, as well as in New England, was becoming intellectual and sterile. The whole dimension of healing was neglected. The experience of personal wholeness by the individual parishioner was not understood. What the Great Awakening had done earlier, the evangelists of the day failed to do then; and people flocked to the heresy propounded by Mary Baker Eddy. Much of today's fad for psychology in the pulpit can be attributed to the same point: the inability to know forgiveness as a real experience. Thus men are led not to reformation but to heresy.

What follows is written not only as a theological but as a parish protest. Karl Barth observed that all theology is church theology. With that, there is no quarrel here. Others have pointed out that the seminary is not an institution set over against the church; it is a part of the church. The seminary is the place wherein the church is able to talk to itself and God in dialogue. This point is also well taken. If it is not true in practice, surely it ought to be.

The protest is, however, that church theology often seems to become obsessed with the position of the theologian. Happily, the reconstruction of seminary curricula seems to be moving us away from the days when all true theology meant either Biblical theology, systematic theology, or historical theology — depending on who was giving the lecture. (Practical theology never was in danger of being considered theological!) Today we almost identify church theology with the official board that pays our salary. For the man who writes from the parish, church theology really means the local church. For the man who is with a board or agency of a denomination, church theology really means Christian education, promotion, missions, or pensions. Any pastor can testify to this by the flood of mail that comes across his desk. Each epistle presents the case for this agency or that board with passion and persuasion. Each time he reads it, the pastor is sure that he has read *the* concern of church theology — until he opens the next letter from another board. The man who writes from the perspective of the seminary often implies that the only real thinking that goes on is the thinking at the seminary. Candidly, he may be right, but that is all the more reason why that man must be on his guard lest he identify church theology with seminary theology.

Recognizing that the previous point is partly overstated, I would charge that church theology is less identified with the local parish than with any other area of the total church. Most seminaries have lectureships conducted by men from management, labor, psychiatry, and the theater. These are interesting, but how often is a lectureship arranged to bring a challenge from the parish? Ministers are often brought in for " inspiration," but not for a theological challenge. Do not even the people of the pulpit and the pew believe there is a message from the parish?

Lack of this challenge means one of two things. It means either that the structure of the parish is totally irrelevant to the Christian faith and the modern world, or that the parish has failed to make its challenge known. But the parish is not irrelevant. That is my protest.

However, let it not be thought that this protest is only to *other* areas of the church. It is to the people of the parish themselves. It has been easy to write books about the parish. It has been easy to make pious and emotional statements about the local congregation. Yet, in large part, the failure of the parish to be taken seriously is the fault of the congregations and the ministers themselves. We have not been willing to take the time to do the thinking, the speaking, and the writing that makes our challenge worthwhile.

Further, in the history of the last thirty years, there has been a growing body of literature in the field of what is called " pastoral theology." This is a theology in its own right — with a content, a methodology, and a systematic treatment. No one has done more in this area than Seward Hiltner. The difficulty with this development is that everyone who is knowledgeable in the field has done his major training in the hospital context. Of the authorities in this field today, how many can be named who have done their research in the context of the actual parish? With some exceptions, almost everyone is either on a seminary faculty or in some form of institutional chaplaincy. Tribute must be made to the truly pioneer work that has been done by those in the state and general hospital programs. Nevertheless, the time has come to shift from the hospital orientation to the parish orientation. Work and research in the hospitals can and must continue. The talent for research and study must now, however, find a focus in the parish of the inner city, the suburb, the changing community, and the city office and industrial plant if the experience of forgiveness is going to be a living experience in the lives of individuals. The research underlying this book finds its center in the changing community.

This protest is also personal. In a real sense, it must be. One of the conclusions of this study is the importance of forgiveness as a personal experience for anyone who would write in the field of theology. It is interesting to observe how each theologian can point to personal events in his life that in fact shaped his theology. Luther was seeking something to make the church alive to him. He wanted answers to personal questions. His theology grew out of that experience and that search. Karl Barth tells of preaching to people in the midst of the war and finding that he had nothing to say. The search transformed his life and his theology. The result was a theology that, to some of us, was the first taste of the excitement that is in theology. Because of the place of personal experience in the life of a man's thinking, it is one of the presuppositions of my thinking, and a conclusion to which the study of forgiveness points, that every theology must begin with awareness of the place of the personal in the life of the writer.

Upon graduation from seminary, I found myself as the assistant minister in a Philadelphia church that was between the times. The church had been part of a great suburban area. The neighborhood was two years away from its first Negro residents. World War II had been ended only three years. The Korean conflict was about to break out. In that situation, when I called in the home or preached in the pulpit, I found myself asking, " What have I got to say as a minister that anybody else could not say? " After the intellectually stimulating influence of Drs. Barth and Brunner, I found myself asking the same question that the theologians of crisis had asked after World War I. I was still looking for the cutting edge of the Christian faith. More than that, I found that my contemporaries were making the same search.

The answer came seven years after my ordination while I was serving as pastor of a small church in the apartment dwellings of New York City. There I met the problems of estrangement that are brought into sharp focus by city life. The cutting edge of the Christian faith turned out to be the realization of forgiveness as a personal experience.

Why did I not find this in the theologies, meaningful as they were? Why did I not find it in seminary, important a milestone as seminary was? The trouble with theology is that theology can be understood intellectually without ever becoming personal. The fact that that can happen says more about me as a student than it does about either of my two seminaries. In fact, as I look back at the undergraduate and graduate days in seminary, I can see that the experience that I identify with forgiveness did happen to me there. The seminary is indeed part of the church. The failure was that that which was really happening to me never became a part of my awareness. The crisis of the city parish succeeded where the security of the seminary failed precisely because it forced into my awareness as a personal experience the realization of forgiveness. This is not to say that that could not have happened in seminary and would always happen in a parish. That was *my* experience. That experience, however, supports the argument of this book: that only when there is opportunity for the realization of forgiveness to become a living part of one's awareness, does the Christian faith have a cutting edge that is relevant to a man's situation.

The protest of this book, therefore, has two purposes. One is to pick up the key term in my previous book, *Divorce, the Church, and Remarriage,* " realized forgiveness." In line with a number of helpful reviews and requests, I now seek to move on to a fuller explanation of what " realized forgiveness " is.

The other purpose, however, is deeper than that. It is to pick up where the previous book ended in an attempt to speak to the church from the perspective of the parish. However, whereas the other book spoke to only one issue in the area of pastoral theology as such, this book seeks to confront the greater scope of theology as a whole. *It is an effort to demonstrate that church theology can be church theology only when the realization of forgiveness is a clear personal experience.*

III ONE SIDE OF CONFESSION

Confession has two sides. One is a negative side. This expresses one's weakness, sin, and need. The other is a positive side. This expresses one's faith. This book is a confession in both meanings of that word. The negative aspect of confession is not an expression of pious humility. The more one gets into an effort such as this, the more one becomes aware of the disadvantage at which a would-be pastor-theologian finds himself. It is not that his work as a pastor is consumed with administration, counseling, and all the details of leading a pastorate. Time-consuming as such functions are, it is that a pastor's reading must generally be geared to his sermon study and to the teaching programs instead of to research. As a result, when he writes, he is very aware of the unread sources in history, theology, and the Bible.

With such a problem, why then does a pastor write? He does so because there is another source with which only a pastor can be fully familiar. That source is the parish itself. No matter who writes, and how authoritative he is, there are areas of knowledge and experience that will have been unexplored by that writer. This is a further reason why church theology must never be identified with any one discipline within the church. It is the reality of this problem which demands that all of church theology must be theology in conversation or dialogue. The situation requires that there always be a two-way conversation between the disciplines simply because of the sources that any one discipline will miss. Therefore the weaknesses do not mean that one should not write. Rather, so far as an individual is concerned, he should speak in order to learn for himself. So far as others are concerned, an individual should speak in order to bear witness to what has happened to him. So far as the whole church is concerned, all should speak and listen; for it is in this way that the awareness of a whole truth, incarnate in Christ, will be revealed to us. That is the presupposition of theological dialogue.

Hence, aware of my own lack of familiarity with the latest book on the New Testament or of the fullest understanding of the early and later church fathers, I nevertheless feel the legitimacy of speaking to these areas from the perspective of the parish.

This conviction also meets the second reason for a negative confession. The writings of Tillich, Barth, Brunner, Bultmann, and Bonhoeffer have all been meaningful to me. Yet suddenly I find myself at odds with these men. Why? Because even where they speak of forgiveness as important in a theological system, the implication of forgiveness in the nature of theological thought itself has not been stated by them. We find this even in Eduard Thurneysen, who speaks as a pastor. He recognizes the proper relationship between forgiveness and confession. Yet in his *Die Lehre von der Seelsorge* (now in American translation as *A Theology of Pastoral Care*), he fails to follow the implications of his awareness for his understanding of theology. The place of forgiveness as an experience is so significant that it qualitatively changes all theological systems. Unawareness of the place of forgiveness sets every theological system into divergent errors. Yet, to make such a sweeping statement does, indeed, leave one with certain anxieties. It is a bit like attacking motherhood! (Or, remembering Freud, should one say fatherhood?)

There is also some concern in the use of the word "experience." I speak of forgiveness as a personal experience. Immediately, some will say that this word is strictly subjective. It therefore cannot be used as a basis for theological discussion. It will be set aside as having the same weakness as Schleiermacher's word "feeling." It will be rejected as psychologizing just as Paul Lehmann, in his book on forgiveness, sets aside Ritschl.[1]

At this point, the reply can be only that "experience" is not here meant in the same way that Ritschl or Schleiermacher speak. The position of this book finds precisely the same weakness of subjectivity in Schleiermacher, Ritschl, and those who follow, that Paul Lehmann and Karl Barth find. However, simply because the theologians of crisis have not come to terms with the *legitimate* dimension of experience in theological thought, the position of "realized forgiveness" finds *the same* error in neo-orthodox and most evangelical theologians as in the liberals. The understanding that "realized forgiveness" has of the currents of theological thought since the Reformation will be discussed in the fifth chapter.

Ultimately, the anxiety of this negative confession is the anxiety of any new discovery. It has shattered my own conceptions of theology which were quite comfortable. It has meant a rethinking of Scripture, theology, and the nature of the human predicament. This personal breakthrough is something like reaching the summit of the Sierras where one looks down into the Sacramento Valley. Reaching the summit is an exhilarating and triumphant sensation. Yet, reaching the summit means only that the whole valley must now be explored. The real work still lies ahead. The excitement of the moment is the knowledge that the new victory gives a basis for examining the valley.

IV   ANOTHER SIDE OF A CONFESSION

Popularly, confession is thought of only negatively. Yet, there is a positive side of confession. What follows is the confession of affirmation.

The nature of this positive confession is twofold. It says something about the nature of forgiveness itself and it says something about the nature of theological thinking. Since the insights for both grew out of my experience in pastoral care, it is right that we should begin at that point.

A parishioner, whom we shall identify as Mrs. A, asked for a series of interviews. It was my own feeling that a therapist who was a professional and who could see her more than once a week would be more helpful than I. Since none was available, since Mrs. A made it clear that she wanted guidance in working through her own problem, and since she was prepared to accept the limitations that we frankly discussed, I agreed to the conversations. In the seventh interview, I had cause to say at one point, " Would you say that you trust people? " There had been a moment's pause, and she had replied unequivocally, " Yes."

In the midst of the eighth interview, Mrs. A asked if I remembered an incident after church, near the first or second interview. When she had met me at the door, I had perceptibly brightened and said, " Hello there." I vaguely remembered the occasion. " My reaction then," said Mrs. A, " was, ' Boy, that was pretty smart;

you're a real psychologist and are trying to make me feel important.' " Mrs. A then asked if I remembered two weeks earlier when
I had phoned for permission to use part of an interview in something I was writing. "At that time," she went on, " I thought to
myself, ' So that's your game; you won't accept any money, but
now I know what you get out of this.' "

The interview then proceeded as follows:

MRS. A: I would like to tell you something that is not very flattering
to me.

MINISTER: All right.

MRS. A: Last week you asked if I trusted people. (*Pause*) Well, I've
discovered that I don't.

MINISTER: I see.

MRS. A: When you asked, I thought, "yes." Now though, I see that
I'm really on my guard and that I've been that way with you. I
couldn't trust you that you were glad to see me at the church door—
just to see me. And then I realized that it was natural that you would
get something out of talking with people and that there was no reason why you shouldn't.

You know, when this first started, I thought I would enjoy it. I
couldn't think of anything more exciting than telling a man about
me. And then I came to hate it. I'd — I'd say I trusted people in that
I would feel all right about leaving a dollar on the table or something. But now I see a more basic problem — a problem I have now
faced. And I'm wondering. Can I really change?

MINISTER: You are seeing a basic problem for the first time; and if I
understand your enthusiasm, you not only wonder if you can really
change, you'd like to.

MRS. A: (*Pause*) Yes. And you know, this reality began to hit me last
week. I began to see I was beginning to trust you. And I went out
of here feeling good — quite free. (*Pause*) But I mean with other people, people in general. Will I get over this? Will my symptoms stop?

Unfortunately this interview was not recorded. I wrote it down
right after the hour because it struck me forcibly. Later, in discussing this episode with Mrs. A, she confirmed the above as in
accord with her memory of the experience.

Something happened in this interview. Mrs. A's problem need
not be diagnosed here. Significantly, she had come to see one
aspect of her problem — and a fundamental aspect of it — which
she had not seen before. This insight was entirely new. It grew

out of the interview. I had not seen it as a basic point. I in no way suspected that the reflective question of the week before would lead to this point. The significant event was that Mrs. A came to a new and creative discovery herself. Why? Because, I would argue, in the context of the pastoral experience, forgiveness became real to her. The word was never mentioned, but the experience was there.

Eduard Thurneysen says that the call to repentance is necessary if forgiveness is to become real. To this, one must ask, " What makes it possible to hear the call to repentance? " In the experience of Mrs. A, it was not repentance that led to a sense of forgiveness. It was the experience of forgiveness which led not only to the ability but also to the desire to ask, " Can I really change? " As will be shown in the following chapter, the realization of forgiveness is not bound to repentance in the way Dr. Thurneysen has put it.[2]

For this reason, I define pastoral care as the mediation of that forgiveness which makes it possible to receive the Word and to repent. The danger in much pastoral work is that the pastor sees his task as that of mediating the Word directly. In preaching, in counseling, and in administration, the pastor does not himself mediate the Word. Rather, he creates the condition in which the Word of God can be mediated. That condition is forgiveness.

What then is " realized forgiveness "? In my previous book, I defined " realized forgiveness " " as the awareness of forgiveness to such a degree that a person is free from the guilt he feels." [3] This definition still holds, and its relation to marriage I would still defend. For the total Christian life, however, I would now define " realized forgiveness " in positive terms. I would now define it as the experience that leaves one free to be creative. In Pauline terms, " *realized forgiveness* " *is the freedom to be a new creature and a new creator.*

In contrast to a key word in counseling, it will be seen that this forgiveness is not just acceptance. Acceptance may be one of the ways in which forgiveness is communicated. However, to be free to accept means that one has set aside feelings of guilt or hate. Forgiveness is a precondition of acceptance. It is at this point that Martin Marty is absolutely correct when he speaks of forgiveness as a discipline — *The Hidden Discipline*. What makes it a different discipline from the Ten Commandments, though, is not, as he asserts, that forgiveness is hidden and the commandments are overt. Rather, it is that forgiveness is a dynamic experience, whereas the laws are of a legal orientation. It is a law of Christ — but a dynamic law. It is what makes the legal law possible (I come not to destroy but to fulfill the law, said Christ) . Forgiveness is a requirement for the individual with regard to himself, because it is what frees him to be personally creative. Without forgiveness, one will die personally. Forgiveness is a requirement in relation to others because it is the only way in which another person can be free and creative. In short, it is the only way that he can be saved. Forgiveness is a requirement both for oneself and for others because that is the only way that true relationships can take place.

In this connection, I recall the first meeting of the World Council of Churches at Amsterdam. Reinhold Niebuhr was delivering his address and made the observation that people are always saying, " If we would just have a little more love in the world . . ." Said Dr. Niebuhr, " that is just the point; how do you love? " The answer is in forgiveness. It is forgiveness that gives the freedom for love.

Further, the interview with Mrs. A suggests something about the nature of the dynamics of forgiveness. Since the word " forgiveness " was never used, forgiveness is not to be identified with just a word or a phrase. Rather, forgiveness appears to be a context that can be expressed by an attitude as well as by a word or a phrase. This is in direct contrast to the position expressed by Martin Marty. In the introduction to his book on forgiveness, Dr. Marty says that his book is written on the assumption that " by the working of the Holy Spirit, the forgiveness of sins can be the generating center of the ethical and moral life." [4] With that point we agree. He precedes it, however, by saying:

The argument is heard that one must begin with the creed, begin with Christ and all His benefits. Luther believed that man must first know what he should or should not do; then, when he is at a loss, he must know where to turn; third, he must have a means of seeking, finding, and enlarging on this strength. *Decalogue comes first in the hidden dis-*

cipline. Whatever may be a good means on a mission to a non-Christian culture, our own culture has been promised so much, has been so over-comforted, overgraced, that we must begin with the demand and judgment of God in order to participate in the joy of the Gospel (Italics mine) .[5]

I believe that the evidence is just to the contrary. Decalogue does not come first in hidden discipline. This is the same error as that of Dr. Thurneysen in holding to the need of repentance first. In the case of Mrs. A it was, again, the context of forgiveness that made any sense of judgment possible. The opposite of " overgracing " or " overcomforting " is not " decaloging " — if I may coin a word — but forgiving. I believe it is the evidence not only of pastoral care but also of the Scripture and the early church that this is so. I believe that the Scripture and the early church see forgiveness as that which is as much related to the judgment of God as the graciousness of God.

What this hypothesis says to the nature of theological thinking is as important as what it says to the nature of forgiveness.

If what follows about " realized forgiveness " is correct, then the relation of pastoral theology to all theology becomes definite. *Pastoral theology becomes the preface or the vestibule to all theology.*

It has been said that logic is the vestibule to theology. From the perspective of systematic theology, there is much to justify this point of view. Logic is a discipline which is necessary for theology. The whole question of epistemology is involved in logic. However, if it is true that church theology is more than just systematic theology, and if theology in general is seen to involve more than just the logic of the mind, then *logic* cannot be considered *the* vestibule of theology.

If the position to be presented about " realized forgiveness " is correct, one point is certain. Pastoral theology cannot be thought of as an appendage to theology in general. In the curricula of many seminaries, pastoral theology has been regarded as nothing more than a practical addition. Why the word " theology " was used at all is sometimes hard to understand. The heading was usually " practical theology," but it would more honestly have read " practical techniques." For these courses, as described, seldom had any content. Instead, they were courses on the level of a trade school. They discussed the art of preaching, how to conduct a funeral, church administration, and, perhaps, psychology. The course had to do with the types of services a minister rendered and seldom if ever were understood as having any theological dimension at all.

If, however, the realization of forgiveness is at the heart of pastoral theology, then it is no longer sufficient to think of pastoral theology after the manner of practical techniques. Operational techniques will be involved, but they will not be the center of the discipline known as pastoral theology. They will be the tools — just as the study of language is a tool for Biblical theology.

More than anyone else, Seward Hiltner has demonstrated the truly theological nature of pastoral theology. His book *Preface to Pastoral Theology* describes pastoral theology as that which stands in a two-way relation to the other theological disciplines. It informs those disciplines and is informed by them. Dr. Hiltner sees theological thought as standing in two great parallel disciplines. One is the " logic-centered " discipline. This involves ethics, historical theology, Biblical theology, dogmatic theology, and philosophical theology. The other great parallel is that which he terms the " operational " discipline. This involves three areas, one of which he identifies as the shepherding area. When Hiltner speaks of pastoral theology, he is speaking strictly of this shepherding function.

Although it builds upon the pioneering work of Hiltner, this book is written from a different perspective. The desire here is to find that which gives a basis for looking at the " operational " disciplines as a whole and as integrally related to the " logic-centered " disciplines. I relate pastoral theology closely to these " operational " disciplines. Further, pastoral theology, as I use the term, centers not so much on the operation of the minister as upon the operation of the parish as a whole. Since " pastoral " refers to the word " shepherd," my approach may not be considered linguistically sound. However, in view of what will be seen about the dynamics of forgiveness, I believe pastoral theology must be understood in this larger dimension. Otherwise, the dialogue between the " logic-centered " disciplines and the foundation laid by Dr. Hiltner for " operation-centered " disciplines will lose its reality. More than that, without the link between the two afforded by " realized forgiveness," neither the " logic-centered " nor the " operation-centered " disciplines will maintain their characters as genuine theologies. They will become merely academic exercises.

Because the view of " realized forgiveness " leads to this enlarged view of pastoral theology as relating to the parish and not just to the minister, the relation of pastoral theology to the other theological disciplines then shifts. Theology, whether " logic- " or " operation-centered," no longer is to be seen as two great bodies of theological thought that parallel each other and inform each other. Rather, pastoral theology becomes the introduction to the other theological disciplines. Pastoral theology, not logic, is the vestibule by which entrance is made to the total enterprise of church theology.

This view means that we have moved a full one hundred and eighty degrees from the position held as recently as twenty years ago. Until then, pastoral theology was thought of, if considered at all, as that which was tacked to the end of the theological enterprise. The argument of " realized forgiveness " is that pastoral theology must now be moved to the beginning of the theological enterprise.

This position also has the value of making the two-way conversation essential. Only in this way can it truly inform or be informed by the other theological disciplines. In any other position, pastoral theology both ceases to be pastoral theology and ceases really to enter into dialogue with the other disciplines. Otherwise, the dialogue is a happy convenience but not a necessity, for then, both disciplines can stand alone.

It is for this reason that pastoral theology might well be called the prolegomenon to all theology. It is for this reason of a different perspective on all theology that pastoral theology can also legitimately be called " theology in a new key." It is a perspective that is as different in this decade from the neoorthodox approach on the one hand, and the Tillichian or existential approach on the other, as were those approaches from the legalistic theologies.

V CONCLUSION

To my knowledge, the position outlined here has not been expressed directly elsewhere. In the course of this study, however, it has been a source of considerable satisfaction and interest to discover support for the basic premise. This support has been found in divergent sources. Recent developments in the Roman Catholic scholarship on moral theology show a radical, if not revolutionary, shift. These developments amount to seeing that moral theology must be understood first in terms of forgiveness and then in terms of law, and not the reverse. Writings in the areas of apologetics, ethics, and theological method as well as pastoral theology also show the same shift. Although the words may be different because of the language that is peculiar to each discipline, the fundamental insight is the same — the realization of forgiveness is the beginning point for any relevant theological enterprise.

Therefore, although it must be left to others to confirm much of what will be suggested, although what follows will raise questions which I hope other disciplines will answer, and although I give answers which will need to be discussed, what is written is written with the conviction that the time has come to sin boldly. It is no longer a matter of the hour being late and the time short in which the church can speak the relevant Christian message in our day. Rather, the time has already run out. The question is whether or not the institutional church can break out of the ghetto of its existence.

By the power of the Spirit, that break has been made in the past. The reality of the dynamics of forgiveness shows that it can be done again. As pastors, we must help our churches discover how, or our churches will be dead. As Christians, theology will begin from that forgiveness which is the heart of the gospel, or the Christian faith will be irrelevant to the crisis of this age. That irrelevance will say nothing about the faith as it is, but it will say much of the betrayal by us who claim to be of that faith.

2

Forgiveness in People

I INTRODUCTION

In replying to his critics, Arnold Toynbee wrote: " The enterprise of trying to organize a comprehensive study of human
affairs is still in its pioneering stage. The pioneer's task is to open
up the jungle by blazing trails. If he does this well, he will have
opened the way for his successor the surveyor." [1] This statement
is especially true when dealing at the same time with man in relation to himself, his fellow, and his God. In the history of knowledge, scientific method itself is young. In the history of scientific
method, the study of man is an infant. In the history of the study
of man, the relationship of science to the other disciplines of
knowledge is still being argued. What has been done before and
what is represented in this book is only a beginning.

In view of this beginning stage, it is important to be clear about
what is and is not being said. This particular chapter is a descriptive chapter. It is an answer to a specific question, viz., " What
does it mean in personal experience to say ' I am forgiven ' or
' You are forgiven '? "

Some people will hold that a book on forgiveness should begin
with the Bible. Others will say that it should start with God.
Where else can we find the Christian understanding of forgiveness? I contend that before questions can be asked about forgiveness in the Bible or in theological thought, we must be clear as
to precisely what human experience we mean when speaking of
" forgiveness." Language, terms, and meanings change. Human
experience is ever the same. In the twentieth century, does the
theologian in his study or the parishioner on the street mean the
same thing that is meant by the Bible? Unless the church and
the world describe the same experience by the word " forgive-

ness," the church is talking about nothing relevant.

Every branch of theology and every theologian has to deal with assumptions. They concern the subjective feelings each brings to the Scripture. To demonstrate the point, consider the following theologians.

Paul Tillich and Rudolf Bultmann are examples taken from liberal theologians. Tillich makes clear what he is talking about as a theologian by describing the method of correlation. For him, all systematic theology, whether in Niebuhr, Barth, or Aquinas, has used correlation.

> It has always done so, sometimes more, sometimes less consciously, and it must do so consciously and outspokenly if the apologetic point of view is to prevail. The method of correlation explains the contents of the Christian faith through existential questions and theological answers in mutual interdependence.[2]

Tillich does not deny the subjective. He recognizes it within his framework. The experiences of life cause men to ask certain questions. The contents of the Christian faith are understood as the answers theology gives to these questions. It is this experience of mutual interaction that is the area of systematic theology.

Bultmann meets the problem of subjective experience through demythologizing or — more accurately — remythologizing. According to Bultmann, mankind has always had to speak through myths. The purpose of a myth " is to express man's understanding of himself in the world in which he lives." [3] For Bultmann, a " myth should be interpreted not cosmologically, but anthropologically, or better still, existentially." [4] In this way, Bultmann makes clear what he means. When he writes theologically, he is describing the way in which people express truth and what this " way " teaches about " the Truth." With Bultmann as with Tillich, people may disagree with the way the problem of subjective feeling is met. Nevertheless, to be sure that one is discussing the same point as Tillich or Bultmann, their *approach* must be understood. Otherwise they and those who discuss them are not talking about the same thing.

Barth, Cullmann, and Niebuhr represent a different approach for dealing with the subjectivity that we all bring to any question.

No one would place these men together as having one point of view. Each has made individual and creative contributions to theology that make him distinctive. It is their oneness in dealing with the matter of subjectivity that results in linking them together as neoorthodox. It is here that they unite in their criticisms of men such as Tillich, on the one hand, and Berkhof, on the other.

Whereas Tillich and Bultmann emphasized the place of existence in dealing with subjectivity, the neoorthodox begin with emphasis on the " Word of God " as the starting point. Dr. Barth writes:

There would be no dogmatics and there would perhaps be no theology at all, unless the Church's task consisted centrally in the proclamation of the Gospel in witness to the Word spoken by God.[5]

Simply because man is subjective, only the grace of God can bring a true knowledge of Scripture and theology.

Reinhold Niebuhr made the point even more bitingly when he wrote in criticism of John Dewey:

It never occurred to him that his insistence that the "method of science " could be transferred from the field of nature to that of history, and that only the intrusion of irrelevant religions and political authority prevented this consummation, rested upon an erroneous and unexamined presupposition. That was the universally held belief of modern culture that the realm of history was essentially identical with the realm of nature.[6]

For Niebuhr, modern science and modern psychology are not adequate to the task of describing the self because the self moves " above the level of social cohesion which may be observed objectively." [7] Therefore, these men dealt with subjectivity by defining theology in terms of that which could be known only by faith — viz., God.

At the far extreme from Paul Tillich is Berkhof. There are great differences among the very conservative just as among the liberal and the neoorthodox. As with Dr. Barth, the conservatives and fundamentalists insist on the Word of God as the given and the starting point. Unlike Dr. Barth, they see this Word of God as concretely identified with the words of the Bible. Therefore, the subjectivity in each of us is met by asking the question, "What does the Bible say?"[8]

Unfortunately, not every pastor is as careful in dealing with the question of his subjective feelings and motives as are the theologians. In a seminar a certain minister submitted a statement of his faith. Upon then being asked how he would deal with a pastoral situation of suicide, he suddenly discovered that the theology by which he lived and the theology he preached were not the same. For this study to be free of that mistake, it must be clear that what follows is based on an assumption.

What is the assumption? It is that there is a basis of relationship between research in the nature of personality and research in theology. This is not to say that Niebuhr is wrong when he states that the personal self moves above that " which may be observed objectively." This fact, however, does not rule out a relationship between the self and " that which may be observed objectively." If the doctrines of the creation and the incarnation mean anything, it must follow that there is some degree of relationship between the visible and invisible.

Later, answer will be given to the positions of Eduard Thurneysen, Karl Barth, and Paul Lehmann who see no basis for assuming this relationship as it will be developed in this chapter.[9] At this point, it is sufficient to observe that the approach of this chapter *is not* the approach of Ritschl, Schleiermacher, and Hermann which is devastatingly analyzed by Barth. Barth surely is correct in rejecting the attempt to build a theology on " feeling " as in Schleiermacher. However, does that rejection mean that there are no human feelings that accompany one's relation to God? Clearly that is not his meaning. The attempt of this chapter is to discuss those feelings insofar as they can be discussed. There are other books — a growing number, in fact — that deal with " forgiveness " from the point of view of the systematic or Biblical theologian. They deal with that dimension of forgiveness which cannot be observed objectively. Theologically, these books are often sound; but they are also largely academic. So thorough has been the rejection of Schleiermacher's " feeling " and Ritschl's " values " that these books do not touch the dynamic fact of what actually happens to a person in the experience of forgiveness.

They say nothing of what Christian forgiveness means when realized in the life of the individual.

The purpose of this chapter, then, is to describe human personality in given situations. By relating certain questions and answers to this description, the goal is to ascertain what it means to say, " I am forgiven." The purpose of the book as a whole will be to see what this description from parish life says about the church's changing views of forgiveness. To do this, we must begin with three specific issues:

1. Is there a correlation between the experience of forgiveness as a part of one's life and the description of personality as integrated and whole? In short, is there a relation between the whole person and the forgiven person? (This is the first question of the present chapter.)

2. What is the correlation between forgiveness as understood in the history of the church and that experience which will be identified with the experience of forgiveness? (A definition of forgiveness is given in this chapter. This question will then be dealt with in Chapters 3, 4, and 5.)

3. Is there anything significant here for the whole matter of theological thought, Christian worship, and the work of the church? (This question will be the focus of Chapter 6. The point is not to define what Biblical, systematic, moral, historical, philosophical, and pastoral theologies are. That problem is for those competent in each field. This third question is to ask whether or not there is something fundamental in all theology and for every method of theology that emerges from pastoral theology.)

Research in the local parish has given rise to the following hypotheses:

1. There is a positive correlation between forgiveness as experienced and personality as integrated or adjusted.

2. The contextual nature of the church is that of forgiveness. This hypothesis is based on a study of a book by Seward Hiltner and Lowell Colston in relation to my research. The book is entitled *The Context of Pastoral Care*. The authors begin by the assertion, with which I agree, that a " minister stands for and represents a kind of understanding that accepts each person ini-

tially just where he is," [10] and that this results in a certain context. They then go on to describe this context in terms of setting, expectation, shifts in relationships between client and counselor, and aims and limitations. [11] These descriptions, however, are comparative. They are a basis for describing pastoral counseling in comparison with counseling in a nonchurch setting. They do not define the nature of the pastoral context in and of itself. My study defines that nature as " forgiveness."

3. The heart of the experience of forgiveness in this day is freedom. Perhaps the most meaningful discovery of this research is the place of freedom in the experience of forgiveness. In all ages, this freedom is seen as freedom to be creative. In different ages, however, the key word or symbol for describing the experience has varied. For Bunyan the important image was that of the lifting of a weight. Today conversation shows that people use the word " forgiveness," but by it they usually have in mind the sensation of freedom.

4. The freedom that a man receives in forgiveness allows him to get " worse " as well as " better." This is not a contradiction of the first hypothesis. Rather, it is saying that where forgiveness is concerned, the accepted or business-world norms of success and failure do not apply. They are inadequate for describing the situation. The indication is that a man may be " worse " in the eyes of the world, yet more mature or " saved " as a person.

5. Forgiveness, to be real, has to have a meaningful instrumentation. This hypothesis means that it is not enough to speak of forgiveness as a context. There also has to be an instrument that brings that forgiveness into the awareness of each person.

These five statements are called hypotheses because the research presented in this chapter by no means proves them. In analyzing what follows, we must be careful not to claim more for the tests and the interviews than is really valid. Simply because Niebuhr is right and there is no one-to-one equation between personality and what can be tested, the conclusions can be no more than tentative. Beyond that, even what can be tested has not been proven conclusively. One man in a parish has neither the financial resources nor the time to do the type of research that would be statistically conclusive. However, there is enough data to make certain definite but *tentative* statements. It will be for any who are interested — be they graduate students or foundations — to test the implications of these conclusions.

II THE BACKGROUND OF RESEARCH

Although it is true that a book such as this is written in the beginning stage of the relationship between scientific and theological thought, a study today is not written in a vacuum. There is a considerable body of research that forms a background. There are many tools of research that are tried and true. It would be possible to begin with the whole psychoanalytic movement. The psychoanalytic schools have developed and refined techniques not only of analysis but also of training and research. The same can be said of the " offspring " of Jung and Adler. Perhaps no more astounding development has come than in the field of psychological testing. The value placed on the testing devices has come under severe criticism of late. Industries and colleges are accused of making too much use of them. These criticisms serve to demonstrate how widely testing has become accepted. There are those who abuse them, but those of us who are outsiders cannot avoid being impressed with the accuracy and the helpfulness of the refined tools that psychologists are making available. Used as an aid and not as the total answer, they can be of amazing value.

Whether in the fields of analysis, psychology, or sociology, there is a general view that each personality can achieve an integrity that might well be called healthy adjustment. There is some disagreement on the nature of personality; but there is no disagreement in psychology about the reality of personality. In addition, some of the evidences of a healthy personality can be described by the various disciplines and schools of thought.

The concern here, however, is not to choose one view of personality against another. Rather, the purpose is to find a unified testing approach that gives a picture of integrity and adjustment. We want one that will serve as representative of the fields of science.

One of the most useful of these is the " Q-sort test " — particularly that developed, used, and reported in the book *Psychother-*

apy and Personality Change (edited by Dr. Carl R. Rogers and
Dr. Rosalind F. Dymond) .[12] The value of this particular instrument is that it was " checked out " for results by people of viewpoints other than those of Carl Rogers. Put roughly, what these
different therapists described as an integrated personality, this
instrument describes as such. It is not related to the philosophy
of Rogers alone. The instrument was developed to test whether
or not Rogers' views were sound, not the reverse. This aim at
universality is what makes it particularly valuable here.

For the record, it should be noted that Rogers would define a healthy personality as one in which all the experiences a
person has had have been dealt with adequately by the individual.[13] Although I, with many other ministers, am much indebted
to Rogers for his insights and understanding of therapy, I think
that his theory does not fully come to terms with the demonic in
life. I think that Rogers' philosophy is wrong when he identifies
any change within a person on a strictly humanistic basis. (What
he often identifies with the power of the self could, and in my
judgment should, be identified with the Holy Spirit.) Nor do I
agree with the basic dictum of his research " that ' anything that
exists, exists in some quantity and can be measured.' " [14] That
position ultimately assumes that everything is three-dimensional.
Such an assumption is questionable and unprovable. Despite
these points of disagreement, Dr. Rogers has made unquestionably helpful discoveries about the nature of personality. He is a
competent therapist himself; and he has contributed much to the
technique of research. Hence, the use of the Q-sort test is generally well accepted.

What is a Q-sort test?

A Q-sort test is a series of statements. Each statement is placed
on a numbered card. The person who takes the test is asked to
place the cards in eight piles on a straight line. In the pile at one
end he is to place the one card that he considers most descriptive
of himself. At the other end he places the card least descriptive.
At the second point from each end, he places four cards, and so
on. In this way, studying and scoring the test will give a picture of
how he would describe himself. The same person may then be

asked to arrange the cards to indicate how he thinks other people would describe him or how he thinks he would want to be described. The difference between the way a person sees himself and the way he thinks he ought to be seen indicates the degree of tension within the person. The closer the score on a person's description of himself and his hopes for himself, the greater the adjustment is considered to be.

In the development of this test, Dymond reports that one hundred cards were given to two well-trained clinical psychologists.[15] They were asked to place the cards in two piles. One pile was to be where the " well-adjusted " person would put the cards that described or were like him. The other pile was to be where the well-adjusted person would put the cards that did not describe, or that were unlike, him. In doing this, these two came to agreement on seventy-four out of the one hundred cards. The cards on which they disagreed were discarded. These remaining seventy-four were then given to four other judges. Their agreement was so high that at no time was there a difference of more than four cards.

In my own use of these same seventy-four cards, over two hundred sortings have revealed a tremendous amount of agreement as to what would be described as a well-adjusted person. Except for one person who took the test just prior to losing touch with reality, no one varied by more than ten cards. (And this particular person, who was entering a psychotic episode, cast the cards with a variance of only twelve.)

In the course of a research program at the Counseling Center of the University of Chicago, this test was given before therapy, at the end of therapy, and six months after therapy had been terminated. At the same intervals, the test was also given to a control group — that is, a group of people who were not undergoing therapy. The results of this program can be found in the book edited by Rogers and Dymond.

For the purposes of the study that follows, the value is that the Q-sort test results were checked by having the same people tested by other measuring devices. The Rorschach and the Thematic Apperception tests were used. The result was a high degree of correlation. It is because of this high correlation that the Q-sort test was taken as an adequate tool for the purpose of checking personality change.

A second piece of research that serves as background for the present study is the Hiltner-Colston work referred to above.[16] In trying to test the hypothesis that personality change progresses slightly faster and farther, other things being equal, in the context of the church than of the secular Counseling Center, the authors came to the following conclusion:

> On the basis of general congruence of findings from the TAT and the Butler-Haigh Adjustment Test, which are roughly in agreement with the counselor's ratings both of change and of outcome, it can be said that the validity of our hypothesis is given some suggestive support and is just on the edge of being statistically significant in the sense that the comparatively greater collective progress of the people at the church could not have been produced by chance. It is only on the edge, however; it is not proved.[17]

The authors go on to say that they were surprised that the data demonstrated as much as it did, and somewhat relieved that it did not suggest more. They are concerned that readers not jump to the conclusion that clergymen can help nearly everybody better than anybody else can help them. They point out that the hypothesis was not about what the clergyman could do, but what the clergyman could do in a pastoral setting as opposed to a nonpastoral setting.

In making this study, Dr. Colston used the testing instruments mentioned in the quotation and compared them both with his own evaluation and with the evaluation of the people he counseled.

The guarded nature of the authors' conclusion is justified not only on the basis of statistics with regard to the people counseled but also because only one person did the counseling. Future tests are needed to see what happens when other clergymen counsel in the different contexts. Further, examples also need to be taken with nonclergymen doing counseling in the different contexts. As a beginning, Dr. Colston's research is sound. Until the same procedure is followed with therapists who are not ministers, however, an important question remains unanswered, viz., " To what degree is *familiarity* a factor in making the clergyman a better counselor in the pastoral context than in the nonpastoral context? " The recording of the counselor's attitude to the people involved does not answer the question as to whether or not the counselor himself would feel freer in one context than in the other. Dr. Colston has made a significant and excellent beginning. It is to be hoped that others will take the research procedure he developed and apply it to the other dimensions of the subject.

Despite the guarded approach of the authors, the Hiltner-Colston report gives some information that is conclusive. Beyond question, it is clear that context is a factor in personality change. This factor is background information which cannot be ignored. It means that whatever is said about the relation of forgiveness to personality must take cognizance of context.

Further, granted the tentative nature of Dr. Colston's research, his book provides grounds for an assumption. The tests dealing with forgiveness will assume that, clinically, there is something about the nature of the church that can make a difference in an individual. The question is, Is this " something " just a psychological or emotional matter, or does the church have something to offer as the church? If we take seriously the point that not everything that is real is testable, we cannot test the nature of forgiveness in and of itself. We can test, however, what the experience of forgiveness is for the individual. We can test whether or not that experience is in any way related to personality change.

III THE NATURE OF THE PRESENT RESEARCH

The present research used three tools. One was the Q-sort test with the addition of cards that related specifically to the question of forgiveness. The second was the recorded interview. The third was a " shift of feeling " test.

The Q-sort test was the one developed by the Counseling Center at the University of Chicago and reported above. Because of the high correlation between the Q-sort test and the TAT in indicating personality change, the TAT was not used here. In addition to the cards in the Q-sort test, seven, then eight, cards were added that pertained directly or indirectly to the way in which people understood forgiveness.

It was mentioned earlier that words have different meanings in different times. Therefore, it is important to identify what experience people have in mind when they speak of forgiveness. To do this, counselees were asked to write brief statements that indicated what they meant. In confirmation classes, one of the questions given to the young people was, " What does it mean to you to be forgiven? " Phrases from psychological and theological books were also studied. Out of these, the seven statements were chosen as the ones most often and universally identified in describing the experience of forgiveness. For purposes of identity I call them the " forgiveness cards."

Subsequently, after many tests had been given, reading in the writings of the early church fathers suggested another word. As will be seen in the chapter on the early church, the Eastern church leaders seemed to concentrate on a different word for the experience of forgiveness than the word itself. This was the word " freedom." A study of the transcript of the recorded interviews made it obvious that the word " freedom " was also constantly used by counselees as something that was desired as much as security. Interestingly enough, when defining forgiveness, these same people seldom mentioned freedom as a part of that experience. Yet, in describing the experience they were after, they used the word " freedom." The realization of the dimension of freedom in relation to forgiveness is one of the most fruitful parts of this research. It was therefore added to the cards.

In this particular test, the counselee was instructed to place the Q-sort cards after the manner of a normal curve with the descriptive cards at one end and the nondescriptive at the other. After he had placed all the cards, he was told to take the " forgiveness cards " and place them anywhere he wanted without regard for the Q-sort distribution. He could place all of them near one pile if he wished.

Thus, a typical distribution of cards would be as follows:

		LEAST LIKE ME			MOST LIKE ME		
Pile No.	1	2	3	4	5	6	7	8
No. of cards	1	4	11	21	21	11	4	1
Forgiveness cards				a,b	c,d	e,f		g,h

In some instances, the " forgiveness cards " would be placed all in one category. In other instances they were spread from pile No. 1 up. For purposes of quick identification, the Q-sort cards were numbered exactly as presented in the Chicago project. The " forgiveness cards " were identified by letter. Hence a counselee was instructed to place the numbered cards in accord with the Q-sort pattern and the lettered cards in any way that he wished.

The counselee was asked to cast the cards three times: first in answer to the question, " What am I like? "; second, in answer to the question, " What do others think I am like? "; third, in answer to the question, " What should I be like? " At the outset of the research, counselees were also asked to have a relative or close friend place the cards the way they thought the counselee would place them and with one added question, " What do I think he (she) is like? " This procedure was soon discarded. In the instances where it was done, it was helpful and revealing so far as the problem of communication is concerned among friends and family members. It is also a good tool for studying the projection of ideas. However, it contributed nothing new about the relation between the realization of forgiveness and personality change. Hence, because it was too time-consuming and difficult to find people to do it, the procedure was stopped. The purpose of the different sortings was to see if a shift in the Q-sort cards would be accompanied by any significant shift in the " forgiveness cards." To the degree that the Q-sort test is an indication of personality adjustment and the " forgiveness cards " are an indication of the dynamic experience of forgiveness, to that degree a comparison of the two sets of cards indicates whether or not there is any type of relationship between the experience of forgiveness and personality adjustment.

The Q-sort cards that would be expected on the " like me " or " unlike me " sides of the pattern are as follows:

UNLIKE ME		LIKE ME	
Item No.	Statement	Item No.	Statement
2 . . .	I put on a false front.	4 . . .	I make strong demands on myself.

UNLIKE ME		LIKE ME	
Item No.	*Statement*	*Item No.*	*Statement*
6 . . .	I often feel humili-ated.	5 . . .	I often kick myself for the things I do.
7 . . .	I doubt my sexual powers.	9 . . .	I have a warm emo-tional relationship with others.
13 . . .	I have a feeling of hopelessness.	11 . . .	I am responsible for my troubles.
16 . . .	I have few values and standards of my own.	12 . . .	I am a responsible person.
18 . . .	It is difficult to con-trol my aggression.	15 . . .	I can accept most so-cial values and stan-dards.
25 . . .	I want to give up try-ing to cope with the world.	19 . . .	Self-control is no problem to me.
28 . . .	I tend to be on my guard with people who are somewhat more friendly than I had expected.	22 . . .	I usually like people.
32 . . .	I usually feel driven.	23 . . .	I express my emo-tions freely.
36 . . .	I feel helpless.	26 . . .	I can usually live comfortably with the people around me.
38 . . .	My decisions are not my own.	27 . . .	My hardest battles are with myself.
40 . . .	I am a hostile person.	29 . . .	I am optimistic.
42 . . .	I am disorganized.	33 . . .	I am liked by most people who know me.
43 . . .	I feel apathetic.	35 . . .	I am sexually attrac-tive.
49 . . .	I don't trust my emo-tions.	37 . . .	I can usually make up my mind and stick to it.

UNLIKE ME		LIKE ME	
Item No.	*Statement*	*Item No.*	*Statement*
50	It's pretty tough to be me.	41	I am contented.
52	I have the feeling that I am just not facing things.	44	I am poised.
54	I try not to think about my problems.	47	I am impulsive.
56	I am shy.	51	I am a rational person.
59	I am no one. Nothing seems to be me.	53	I am tolerant.
62	I despise myself.	55	I have an attractive personality.
64	I shrink from facing a crisis or difficulty.	61	I am ambitious.
65	I just don't respect myself.	63	I have initiative.
69	I am afraid of a full-fledged disagreement with a person.	67	I take a positive attitude toward myself.
70	I can't seem to make up my mind one way or another.	68	I am assertive.
71	I am confused.	72	I am satisfied with myself.
73	I am a failure.	74	I am likable.
76	I am afraid of sex.	75	My personality is attractive to the opposite sex.
77	I have a horror of failing in anything I want to accomplish.	78	I am relaxed, and nothing really bothers me.
83	I really am disturbed.	79	I am a hard worker.
84	All you have to do is just insist with me,	80	I feel emotionally mature.

UNLIKE ME		LIKE ME	
Item No.	*Statement*	*Item No.*	*Statement*
	and I give in.		
85 . . .	I feel insecure within myself.	88 . . .	I am intelligent.
86 . . .	I have to protect myself with excuses, with rationalizing.	91 . . .	I am self-reliant.
90 . . .	I feel hopeless.	94 . . .	I am different from others.
95 . . .	I am unreliable.	96 . . .	I understand myself.
99 . . .	I am worthless.	97 . . .	I am a good mixer.
100 . . .	I dislike my own sexuality.	98 . . .	I feel adequate.[18]

The reader might disagree with some of these statements. For example, Statement 72 reads, " I am satisfied with myself." Is it healthy to be satisfied with oneself? If this statement means that a person does not feel a compulsion to " keep up with the Joneses," few would question it. Considered in other ways, however, it might be debated. Similarly, in the course of giving this test, some people have asked, " Was this written for young people? " They would point to the question about being attractive to people of the opposite sex. " When I was younger, that would have been important; but at my age I'm not particularly concerned about it."

These comments underscore the importance of understanding and using the Q-sort test properly. The above division is not a description of what *is* healthy adjustment but of the way most people describe that adjustment. Further, the test is used by way of comparing people not with this particular standard but with the standard that they have picked themselves. Thus people are asked to place the cards at least twice: once to describe themselves and once to describe what *they* consider to be the norm. The Q-sort test is not a device for comparing people with other people. It is, rather, what Gordon Allport calls an " idiographic " test. It is something that describes a person within himself.

In the above test, it will be noted that the numbers of the statements do not run from 1 to 100. The missing numbers are the ones that were discarded because the judges did not agree on them when the test was developed.

The "forgiveness cards" that were added to be used in connection with the Q-sort test are as follows:

ITEM NO.   STATEMENT

a........I am forgiven.
b........People forgive me.
c........I can accept people as they are.
d........I am the kind of person people can accept.
e........I am liked.
f........God loves me.
g........I love God.
h........I feel a sense of freedom.

Whether or not everyone who used these cards agreed with every statement as descriptive of the realization of forgiveness in his or her own life is not important. What is important is that most people would identify one or more of these statements as "like me" when they described the experience of feeling forgiven. What we are talking about when we speak of forgiveness as a reality in a person's life is to some degree expressed by these statements. Other statements could also be used. Some people prefer the word "care" to the word "love." Nevertheless, what is given here has proven adequate for the research to this point.

The scoring of these tests is rather simple because the main question of the test is one of correlation between the two sets of statements. A more elaborate and more precise form of scoring is necessary when speaking to aspects of personality change that are discussed in the Chicago study and that by Dr. Colston. That procedure and formula can be found explained at length in those publications.

Here, the value of the Q-sort test was to see what items were shifted from the "like me" to the "unlike me" side (and the reverse), to see if any particular item made a spectacular jump, and to have a scale for rating the "forgiveness cards."

The scoring was done simply by assigning one point to each item that corresponded with those which were placed on the "unlike me" and the "like me" sides of the curve. Thus, if in describing himself, a person placed forty of the cards on the sides that corresponded to the table, the score would be 40-74. There are seventy-four cards, and he placed forty of them after the same manner as the judges did. In and of itself, this would tell nothing. In answer to the question, "What should I be like?", assume that the same person placed the cards at such agreement that the score came out 70-74. This would indicate a great difference between what the person thought he was and what he thought he ought to be. This would indicate considerable inner tension and lack of adjustment.

The result of the Chicago test showed that in therapy it is possible for the personality to change so that a new reading of the score might well be 60-74 for one's picture of himself and 70-74 for his picture of what he ought to be. That scoring would indicate a person with less inner turmoil, less tension, and a greater degree of adjustment than before.

The "forgiveness cards" are scored by giving a value to each card equal to the number of the pile it is in, and then adding them together. For example, if each card is in the fifth pile, then each card would have a value of five and the total score for the lettered cards would be forty (for all eight cards). If a person felt that all cards described his feeling of forgiveness and that he had that feeling, he would place all cards in pile eight. In that case, his score would be 64.

In a hypothetical case, a man might describe himself in such a way that he put two cards in the fifth pile (ten points), three in the sixth (eighteen points), and three in the seventh (twenty-one points). The total would be 49. In describing what a person ought to feel in terms of forgiveness, the man in question might put all in the last pile for the sixty-four points. If the hunch of the research is correct, the greater one's personal adjustment, the closer will be the score to the total of sixty-four.

These tests were used in three areas: The first was to test what happened in the area of counseling; the second, in the area of public worship (different types of services) ; the third, in the area of an educational experience. In each instance, the question was to see what changes, if any, would be noted over a period of one hour. Hence, the one-hour interview, the one-hour worship service, and the one-hour classroom experience were compared. In addition, the tests were also given at the end of a twenty-four-hour period of time.

For each of these, it was necessary to have a " control." A control is a situation in which no previously planned experience takes place. This control was handled in two ways. After the model of the Chicago experiment, some people were asked to take the tests prior to and after a period of work on the job; others did it in connection with a period of rest; and others in connection with a period of reading. The other control was done by the counselees themselves. In the course of the week, they took the test over a period of time equal to that which elapses in a worship service, a classroom experience, or a counseling hour. This provided a degree of constancy in comparison. It meant that the prime difference in the two sets of tests was between the experience of worship, class, or counseling, and the unplanned experience.

The second tool was the recorded " interview." The word is put in quotes because it refers not only to the specific counseling interview but also to some small-group discussions. These interviews were sometimes in the course of short-term — often one meeting — counseling. In two instances these interviews were matters of counseling for a period of eight months in weekly intervals. The intent of these interviews is to see what took place within the counseling situation. This is also compared with written records of what took place within the worship services and what took place within the classroom situations. The purpose of these interviews was twofold. Initially, there was the attempt to understand what people considered to be the experience of forgiveness. Out of these discussions, the " forgiveness cards " were developed. Subsequently, there was the desire to understand what happened within the interview itself. What happened to the parishioner? What happened to the minister?

The third tool was the " shift of feeling " test. This was developed when it became obvious that one of the problems in the research was the length of time required for a person to take the Q-sort test. To take the test three times, have an hour's counseling or worship, and take it again meant a total of at least four hours at one sitting. Aside from the part that fatigue could play in the results, businessmen, housewives, and students simply did not have that amount of time available.

Since, as will be seen in a moment, it was established early in the proceedings that there was a striking correlation between the use of the "forgiveness cards" and the Q-sort cards, it was decided to set up an instrument that was based on the "forgiveness" categories alone. The purpose was to identify shifts in those categories which reflected the experience of forgiveness. The subject would fill out the sheet prior to the planned experience and an identical sheet after the planned experience. The scores were then compared. By the use of this process and the use of controls, it was possible to establish definite shifts during certain types of experience.

The notable addition in this particular test was the experience of devout members of the Roman Catholic Church. Again I am particularly indebted to the clergy of the Sacred Heart Church in Bloomfield who cooperated in this venture and made it possible for some of the church members to participate.

The shift-of-feeling test was as follows:

Before I attend confession (if Roman Catholic) or a conference with the pastor about a personal matter (if Presbyterian), I often feel

	TO NO DEGREE				TO A GREAT DEGREE			
	1	2	3	4	5	6	7	8
a. I am forgiven.	—	—	—	—	—	—	—	—
b. People forgive me.	—	—	—	—	—	—	—	—
c. I can accept people as they are.	—	—	—	—	—	—	—	—
d. I am liked.	—	—	—	—	—	—	—	—
e. God loves me.	—	—	—	—	—	—	—	—
f. I love God.	—	—	—	—	—	—	—	—

	To No Degree				To a Great Degree			
	1	2	3	4	5	6	7	8
g. I am the kind of person whom people can accept.	—	—	—	—	—	—	—	—
h. I feel a sense of freedom.	—	—	—	—	—	—	—	—
*i. I feel a sense of strength.	—	—	—	—	—	—	—	—
*j. I feel a weight lifted.	—	—	—	—	—	—	—	—

Before I attend a service of worship I often feel

	To No Degree				To a Great Degree			
	1	2	3	4	5	6	7	8
a. I am forgiven.	—	—	—	—	—	—	—	—
b. People forgive me.	—	—	—	—	—	—	—	—
c. I can accept people as they are.	—	—	—	—	—	—	—	—
d. I am liked.	—	—	—	—	—	—	—	—
e. God loves me.	—	—	—	—	—	—	—	—
f. I love God.	—	—	—	—	—	—	—	—
g. I am the kind of person whom people can accept.	—	—	—	—	—	—	—	—
h. I feel a sense of freedom.	—	—	—	—	—	—	—	—
*i. I feel a sense of strength.	—	—	—	—	—	—	—	—
*j. I feel a weight lifted.	—	—	—	—	—	—	—	—

* These two items were added for only the last test group — viz., the volunteers at the young adult conference.

An identical chart was used for checking after the hour. The instructions were changed merely to the point of indicating what should be done " After I attend. . . ."

The scoring was done in precisely the same manner as in the case of the " forgiveness cards."

IV Lessons from the Research

It takes time to explain a testing tool. It takes even longer to use it. Comparatively, it does not take long to present its results. The lesson from the first tool — the Q-sort test plus the " forgiveness cards " — is that there is a striking correlation between the two.

Comparisons were made among one hundred and fifty-three different placements of the Q-sort test and the " forgiveness cards." In one hundred and fifty of these, as the adjustment ratio moved up, the " forgiveness score " went up. As the adjustment ratio went down, the " forgiveness score " went down. A typical example is the case of a graduate student, married, with children, and with part-time employment. His view of what he was like showed a score of 32–74. After counseling, the score had moved to 44–74. The " forgiveness score " had changed from 28 to 38. As the adjustment ratio moved up, so did the " forgiveness score." In response to the question, " What should I be like? " his adjustment ratio was 68–74. His " forgiveness score " was also higher; it was 46.

What about the three tests out of the one hundred and fifty-three that did not follow the pattern? In one there was no change. In the other two there was a slight downward trend. The adjustment score changed slightly, but the " forgiveness score " remained the same. However, it is to be noted that in each of these three exceptions, all the adjustment scores involved were in the 60's and the adjustment shifts were slight.

On the basis of this evidence, I believe it is legitimate to conclude that there is a positive correlation between what people mean when they speak of forgiveness as real and what tests indicate to be good emotional adjustment.

If the first hypothesis is considered legitimate, the question then arises as to the nature of forgiveness. This question is partly answered by the "forgiveness cards," for they reflect what was described in the interviews. It is to the interviews, then, that attention is given for a sense of the nature of forgiveness.

Although ideally the interviews would be presented here in full so that the reader could make his own evaluation, the length of the interviews makes that impossible. What I have seen in the scope of the interviews with various parishioners, however, is portrayed in the story of one man. The following excerpts in which the dynamics can be seen are taken primarily from recorded interviews. Some of the concluding parts were taken from memory because the information came at times and moments when it was impossible to record. The notes were made immediately after the conversations.

Mr. Sim, as I shall call him, has kindly consented to my presenting as much of our relationship as will be helpful. I am particularly appreciative of this, for in many respects this counseling was a failure on my part. Because it was a failure, certain items that I wish to discuss stand out more clearly than in some "successful" instances.

Mr. Sim came to me ostensibly because of a sexual problem. His wife also spoke with me for a number of interviews. The problem was a genuine threat to their marriage. However, both of them wished to save the marriage and meet the problem. Interviews were set on a weekly basis. Despite their concern, desire, and regular attendance at the interviews, I began to be troubled. Although, on the surface, the worst manifestations of the problem had abated, I had the feeling that we were not getting anywhere. Mr. Sim had been coming for over six months, but I felt that the real issue had not been met. As I looked back over the record, it became clear that my schedule for seeing Mr. Sim had had many interruptions. One week there was a funeral. Another week there was a conference that called me out of town. Holy Week was so full that it was necessary to skip our session. With that discovery, and full discussion of the problem with Mr. Sim, we concentrated on a number of interviews prior to vacation.

Before and toward the end of these sessions the Q-sort test and "forgiveness cards" were used by Mr. Sim. The results were not surprising. There had indeed been some shift toward greater adjustment, but the shifts were by no means startling.

Shortly after the end of the vacation, a call came from Mr. Sim's wife. She reported that the sexual manifestations of her husband's problem had returned with full force. In the belief that Mr. Sim could be helped, but only on a far more regular and intensive basis than I had been able to work, I referred him to a clinical psychologist.

About a month after he began his interviews, with the psychologist, Mr. Sim had a religious experience. His wife had felt it necessary to begin divorce proceedings, but Mr. Sim was so overcome by his experience that he was sure all would be well. He was driving along the road, found it necessary to stop because of the rain, and had a vision of Christ that made clear to him that he was forgiven. Out of that experience, he wrote members of his family, his wife, and me. To all of us he said:

The prodigal son, like all the rest of us, for a long time kicked up the dust of self-deceit before " he came to himself " and said, " I will arise and go to my father, and I will say to him, ' Father, I have sinned.' " Today, I went before my God and said, " Father, I have sinned." For the first time I was able to take Communion and honestly believe that I was receiving the body and the blood of Jesus Christ.

After considerable description of his feelings and expression of his confession, Mr. Sim then wrote:

Lo, and behold, the fear of that moment that I had carried so long, not simply faded away, that fear dissipated instantaneously. I found myself and " was born again," nevermore to turn back to myself, but evermore to give out of myself.
This experience was so profound and so real that I immediately understood that it was only a beginning, truly a being born again. And just as surely I know that this new life will be rewarding where the other bore fruit that was poisoned. For, having turned myself out, I have freed myself for expression that was not available to me before — because any expression before would have been false — not as a lie, but simply founded on something which did not exist.

Upon receiving this letter from Mr. Sim, I was overjoyed. Certainly my own feelings of guilt for not having helped him more were assuaged, and I was pleased that he had taken the time to write me of his feelings and experience.

Only one thing was wrong. The sexual problems showed them-selves again, he left home, and all but landed on skid row.

Several months later I met Mr. Sim when he was working as a waiter in a restaurant. He called me aside, spoke for several min-utes, and asked if he could come to see me again and bring me to date on his life.

He said that he had taken to drinking heavily and was literally walking to skid row in lower Manhattan. On several occasions he had passed Grace Episcopal Church. On this particular night, at two in the morning, he went into the church. He sat there for a while, and then saw a sign that said "counseling at any hour." He rang a bell and found that it was true. After talking with the curate, he accepted the advice to go to an Alcoholics Anonymous group not far from where he was then living. "There," said Mr. Sim, "I discovered that my real problem was alcoholism. Since I was in college, not a day went by that I did not have a drink. I have now admitted that I am an alcoholic, I am following the twelve steps, and I feel that I am really making progress. I do not know if I will ever be able to get back with the family, but if that is not to be, I feel that I can take that too."

Inevitably, I asked about his religious experience and whether or not this meant it was not real and that the church had failed. "I like to think it was real," he said, "for it freed me enough from the past to find out what I really was — an alcoholic." The church and the faith he considered relevant, for the church re-ceived him at the critical moment. "The difficulty with the re-ligious experience and the later failure of the church," he went on, "was that there was no way in which I could meaningfully tell them. I could not stand up in the congregation and tell it, but I can tell it in AA. That is what makes the difference."

From a psychological standpoint I would still question whether or not alcoholism was Mr. Sim's basic problem. Rather, it appears that the sexual expressions and the alcoholism were both mani-festations of the problems that relate to what Freud would iden-tify as the oral stage of development. In terms of alcoholism and the AA group, he has found a meaningful handle with which to get hold of the problem. In terms of sex, he could not do it.

What emerges from this biography that relates to our understanding of "realized forgiveness"?

Initially, it is obvious from Mr. Sim's comments that saying one is forgiven cannot necessarily be equated with the experience of forgiveness. I personally do not doubt a dimension of "realized forgiveness" in the mystical experience he had. Yet, clearly it was not the last word. I am sure that my attempt to describe Mr. Sim's experience cannot do justice to the contrast between the man who with great certainty told of his moment in the rain and the man who hesitatingly told of the night on skid row. In the first instance, the word "forgiveness" was freely used. That was it, and he knew it. Yet, as one reads his letter and remembers the confidence of the afternoon, reflection recalls just a hint of Shakespeare's "The lady doth protest too much, methinks." In the quiet humility of the second scene, with its sense of surrender even to the fact that he had not achieved everything yet, there seemed a greater freedom than before. In this second instance, he never once mentioned the word "forgiveness," yet he seemed to have that for which he was seeking.

For what was he looking? All the words used in the "forgiveness cards" are different ways that people have described the experience. In his letter he spoke to the heart of it when he spoke of having "freed myself for expression that was not available to me before." The word "free" was a recurring one throughout the interviews. The following excerpt from the first interview expressed the theme:

PASTOR: Then you feel that whenever you're in a discussion Mrs. Sim gets upset?

MR. SIM: It's part of my unloading and, uh, I try to tell her that if we're going to be pleasant, even though I don't break down and cry or something, it doesn't mean that I don't have emotions. I may be torn up inside, but it just won't show. Uh, sometimes I wish I could cry more, but I just don't.

In this statement, Mr. Sim expresses his problem as not being able to speak. He was not free to express himself. In a subsequent interview, he related this inability to his fear of women:

It all of a sudden seemed to be clear. But I – all of a sudden, it was almost like a – not a light, but an opening of a door, in a way. Uh, I think I've been afraid of women all my life. . . .

Hence, the freedom he would like at this point is freedom from fear of women. Similarly, throughout the interviews, expressions were made of things from which he would like to be delivered — his guilt, his fears, his head and back aches.

Further, the interviews demonstrate that forgiveness dynamically involves more than just the person and more than just a legalistic atonement. Much has been made in other literature about the case of Mrs. Oak and the point where she turned to the therapist and said, " It suddenly dawned on me that in the . . . client-counselor kind of thing, you *actually care* what happens. . . ." The effect of realizing that someone cares is very important. However, what if the pastor fails in his approach? Is it just the counselor's concern that makes the difference? My experience with Mr. Sim suggests that the answer is " No."

After an interview session during which I told him that I had not been feeling well, I listened to the recording of the hour. My inability to be concerned and my unawareness of my own situation reflected itself at every turn. At the next session, therefore, I was quite surprised when Mr. Sim said that he was in better spirits and that the previous interview had been especially helpful. Upon hearing this, I purposely sidetracked the interview to ask for an evaluation of the previous week's experience. Part of the exchange went thus:

PASTOR: I was having throat trouble and all of that may be true, but from the standpoint of real help, I considered it a technically lousy job. And yet you say you feel better. Now I would be interested in your evaluation of last week. Did you feel that I was more difficult than other times, off base, or what?

MR. SIM: Very frankly, I had expected — uh, of course when I came in, I didn't realize your health situation. I think I expected I would get more response from you in regard to what I was saying. However, because of the health factor, I didn't really get too upset. I think that just the self-expression was a major step anyway.

To this I replied that, upon hearing the tape, I had suddenly become aware that he had said something significant, and that I had missed the significance. He then responded with a statement of considerable value here. After an opening sentence he said: " If you had been in good health last week and we had had the

same meeting that we had, I think I would have been quite dis-
appointed. But understanding that you were pretty much under
the weather, I thought, 'Well, after all, you can't expect too
much, really.' "

Two points are important. Initially, the previous interview did
not depend entirely upon the pastor. In the interview quoted
from our first visit, Mr. Sim had expressed a desire to be free to
express himself. By his testimony, in the preceding interview he
experienced some of that freedom. Why? It was not because of
the minister at that point. In fact, Mr. Sim could have felt rejected, and we would not blame him. Instead, Mr. Sim was understanding because an ethos of rapport was there which was *more*
than just the minister. What the minister had done in previous
interviews had helped create that ethos. At that moment, however, what allowed Mr. Sim to progress was beyond the immediate
pastoral contact.

Another feature of this interview was a sudden reversal of roles.
The pastor became the counselee, and Mr. Sim the counselor. It
was Mr. Sim who spoke of understanding the pastor. What he
meant was that he left the pastor free to be what he was — under
the weather. He communicated that freedom by being accepting;
but it was freedom that he gave. What made it possible for this
to take place? Again it was not the person of the pastor alone. An
ethos had been created which made it possible.

This ethos I equate with what Drs. Hiltner and Colston refer
to as context. The context of which Dr. Colston speaks is the context of a freedom to be what one is.

This by no means says that the pastor need pay no attention to
his technique or approach. In listening to the recording of that
interview, I discovered that I began asking Mr. Sim some questions. These questions were couched in such a way that he would
give the answers that I wanted; and then I would congratulate
him on his insight! According to the recording, I suddenly became aware of what was happening, stopped the cat-and-mouse
game, asked Mr. Sim precisely what I wanted to know, and went
on with the business of paying attention to Mr. Sim's concern. As
soon as that happened, a noticeable sense of relief came into
Mr. Sim's voice and he began to move to the statement that was

significant for him. The place of the minister in the interview is this: he is responsible for making real the context of freedom, but he is not that freedom himself.

Not only does forgiveness involve more than the minister, it also involves more than any legal concept of paying the price for wrongs. Freedom did not come simply by the pastor saying, " I forgive you " or " Feel free to be yourself." There was a price for Mr. Sim's wrongs which could be rather easily paid. He had gone into debt; and he could work until the debt was met. Yet, in speaking to the point of forgiveness itself, Mr. Sim said: " Forgiveness in a sense is funny. It's not something you can grab ahold of. If <u>X</u> would not always mention <u>(what happened)</u>, it would somehow suggest forgiveness." After a few exchanges of comments I replied:

PASTOR: I think you're saying that this which happened will always be a part of you and a part of her because it happened. You cannot deny the reality of the experience.

MR. SIM: *(Pause)* Yes. *(Pause)* Yes, I think I'm trying to say that to me, uh, forgiveness is somewhat a — a degree of understanding. *(Pause)* I think I mean not only understanding someone else, but understanding someone else or some other thing in relation to everything else.

PASTOR: I see.

MR. SIM: How big a crime, for instance, was it really? How much of an insult was it really?

PASTOR: In other words, to see it in a truer perspective, not just to know the facts. Is —

MR. SIM: *(Breaking in)* Yes, yes, that's it. It's sort of like people who are sarcastic, and they rub you the wrong way. But when you look at it from the right angle, there are others who can be sarcastic and make you laugh.

PASTOR: Um.

MR. SIM: *(After considerable comment)* . . . To somehow get this in perspective and work on it from there. . . .

Here Mr. Sim is saying that forgiveness is a matter of being free to see things in proper proportion. That is what he meant by " understanding." This is further evidence that, dynamically, forgiveness refers to a context — a context in which one can be free to see things as they are. Forgiveness is not just a matter of balancing books in a ledger.

Further, this interview clearly illustrates that the freedom which comes from forgiveness will not always mean that one will move in the right direction. In his freedom, one may deny the very context of forgiveness, decide that he is master of his fate, and go his own way. This is the sin against the Holy Spirit, for when one rejects the context of forgiveness, one rejects forgiveness itself. The experience of Mr. Sim, after his mystical moment in the rain, showed that he was free to go to the next step; but that step meant not only more clarity about, but more experience *in,* his sin. Like Peter after the Last Supper, so Mr. Sim after Communion denied his Lord. To this point, then, the interviews with Mr. Sim show that there is a contextual nature to the experience of forgiveness. The hallmark of this context is freedom. That it is freedom is shown in the fact that Mr. Sim could go either way. Regardless of what he did, this contextual dimension of freedom must be remembered if the full dynamics of " realized forgiveness " are to be understood.

Out of not only the interview with Mr. Sim, but out of other interviews as well, it is seen that *the context* of freedom *is* only *one dimension of " realized forgiveness." Equally important is the observation that a sense of forgiveness also requires an adequate instrumentation of that context.* There must be some instrument that adequately brings to personal awareness the context of freedom. Thus, in referring to one of his clients, Dr. Colston wrote: " The unaided interpretation of her suffering was not in itself remedial. For it to become remedial there had also to be articulation in just the kind of relationship she found in counseling." So it was also with a young teen-ager. At the beginning of one interview she said, " I have so much to say, but somehow I can't say it." Until she could find an instrument of expressing the context of freedom, she could not realize the forgiveness that was there.

Further demonstration of this point came in the experience of another pastor. At a meeting of his denominational organization, he made a statement that left him feeling foolish and that he felt had been wrong. In talking with his wife, in talking with me, and in talking with the one man who might have been hurt by what he said, he did not find an adequate instrument for making the freedom or the context of forgiveness real. Only when he spoke to the executive officer, that is, the representative of the whole organization, did he experience freedom to move on. " And when I did," this pastor said, " I suddenly found myself making the best suggestions I had ever made before the group."

These instances from the experience of Mr. Sim and from other reports indicate that forgiveness is, indeed, often expressed in terms of freedom. This freedom, however, is made real only when there is that instrumentation which allows for its expression. Somehow the overall dynamics of forgiveness in one's life seem to move continually back and forth between these two elements. As the proper awareness brings the context into reality, that context leads to a deeper awareness which in turn gives expression to a deeper reality. The pages that follow concerning forgiveness in the Bible and in the early church will help sharpen this dynamic picture of forgiveness. Here, the evidence of the research thus far indicates the dynamic nature of forgiveness and the relevance of forgiveness to personality growth. The research does not give us the full picture of forgiveness, but in pointing out the contextual nature and the instrumental nature, and the interplay between them, the research has clarified the picture of what forgiveness is. That is all that it was asked to do.

The third area of the research program concerns what happens in certain specific situations. If the interviews show that forgiveness needs instrumentation, then the question arises as to what the instrumentation is that will make forgiveness real. The Q-sort test with the " forgiveness cards " was used to study some of these matters. In other instances, only the shift-of-feeling scale was used. In these tests, then, we move from seeing forgiveness in the counseling situation to seeing it in other aspects of church life.

Consider those matters tested by the Q-sort test and " forgiveness cards." These tests are not statistically significant in that they do not cover a great span of people. Instead, a few individuals were asked to cover a spectrum of experiences to see whether or not there was a basis for making any type of observation about those experiences.

One pastor took the test in connection with the conduct of a service of worship. His control test, taken after waking on two successive mornings, showed almost no change. The scores on the three questions ("What am I like?" "What do others think I am like?" and "What ought I to be?") were 48–74 (first day) and 48–74 (second day); 62–74 (first day) and 62–74 (second day); and 66–74 (first day) and 70–74 (second day). In regard to each of these three questions, the "forgiveness scores" showed a slight change upward (41 to 45, 43 to 47, and 45 to 48, respectively).

In the test before and after the service, the significant contrast was in the view he had of himself. Before the service, he had a score of 32–74 and after the service a score of 44–74. The fact that both these scores are lower than after he awoke is not significant here because they are not comparable. They would be comparable only if the control cards were cast after he had been up and about for a few hours and already had to face some of the anxieties of the day. It is the difference in shift that is significant. In the control situation, there was no shift. In the test situation, there was a shift of twelve points on the Q-sort test and ten points on the "forgiveness cards" (28 to 38). In the control, the shift was zero on the Q-sort test and four on the "forgiveness cards."

What is the significance of this comparison? It is possible that nothing is seen here but relief from the tension of having to conduct the service. The testimony of the subject, however, is that the service itself was no direct threat, that he used the service as a means of confession, and that he had felt a sense of release after the point of confession in his conduct of the service.

The test was also given to two people to use before and after periods of private meditation. The tests revealed no real change within themselves nor difference between the test situation and the control. This does not say that private meditation cannot be a genuine instrument. The lack of change probably indicates that the Q-sort test is too cumbersome a testing device to be used in connection with a five- or ten-minute period of meditation. It may mean that at given times the private meditation is not significant in relation to the realization of forgiveness. There simply is not enough evidence to judge at this point.

Unexpectedly, one person took the test in relation to a church service and, immediately afterward, in relation to a counseling situation. Although I have the written testimony as to what took place, it is my personal regret that the tests themselves were not available. These tests were taken by a student, and the test results seem to have disappeared with his graduation. The point of interest is that he reported no change of any relevance in connection with the church service itself (a free-church tradition service with little formal liturgy). This was of concern to him, because he entered the church with a genuine problem disturbing him. He found that it was not easy to follow the advertising line, "Take your troubles to church and leave them there." However, after the service — and after he had completed the retake of the test — he had a chance for private conference with the minister. "I felt released and free," he said. He had the presence of mind to cast the cards again. This time there was a significant shift upward both in personality adjustment and in the "forgiveness card" scores. In this instance, he sensed what he felt was an experience of forgiveness not in church but in the private face-to-face relationship with the pastor.

This test does not say that the worship service is not a legitimate instrument for realizing forgiveness. It does say that in some instances, the private relationship is a more adequate instrument.

One student also attended a service of worship that was formal liturgically. It had a printed confession that was used by the entire congregation. There was slight change in these scores. The Q-sort test scores on the three questions stood as follows before and after: (a) 54–74 became 61–74 (the "forgiveness card" shift moved from 50 to 51); (b) 60–74 remained 60–74 and the "forgiveness card" shift moved from 50 to 53; (c) 60–74 remained 60–74 and the "forgiveness card" score remained 56 both times. The control showed no significant shift. It is definite that the test showed an increase in the appraisal of oneself and a complete reduction of tension. After the service, each score was in the area of sixty. The service can be said to have contributed somewhat to an awareness of forgiveness, but the evidence is still slight.

At this point in the research two changes developed. As will be noted, the changes in the forgiveness scores were not great. At the most, only trends could be claimed. This was the point at which I became aware of the word "freedom" as a dimension of forgiveness. A "freedom" card was then added to the "forgiveness cards " and proved to be the most volatile of all the cards.[19] The Q-sort cards would move definitely, but the "forgiveness cards" would move only slightly. The card that read, "I feel a sense of freedom" saw genuine action. Subjects would place it low in their descriptions of themselves and high in their descriptions of what they ought to be. Subjects moved it considerably with regard to the before and after experiences.

The other change was a growing awareness of the cumbersome nature of the Q-sort test for the people involved. Thus, the shift-of-feeling sheet was used.

When still using the Q-sort test, but with the added "forgiveness card" on freedom, I gave the test in two types of classroom situations. In each instance three people took the test. In the first classroom situation I had a group of college students for two hours. The pattern of the session was thirty minutes of lecture followed by thirty minutes of group discussion. There were ten students in all who joined me around a table. The subject was "Marriage and the Family." None of these tests showed any significant change. A typical scoring was (a) 64–74 became 66–74, (b) 58–74 remained 58–74, and (c) 64–74 became 68–74. Each of these students seemed to have a high level of emotional adjustment to begin with. Would it have been different if their evaluations of themselves had been lower?

In the second classroom situation, the approach was straight lecture with freedom to interrupt and to ask questions (a freedom that was greatly exercised). The teacher was a highly personable young man who gave the group of twelve a biweekly Bible study program. Four people undertook the test. These were all people at or near retirement. In these instances the ratios began in the low forties. With three of the people, however, the picture was, as with the college students, one of no substantial change. One person showed a jump of ten points on the personal evaluation of the Q-sort test and eight points on the "forgiveness cards." There was no change in the other two categories.

When I had studied these tests my inevitable conclusion was that the instrument which will make forgiveness real depends both upon the person and upon the situation. Those situations in which there is a consciousness of the need to mediate forgiveness and provide an instrument whereby it can become real seem to succeed to a greater extent than those in which there is not such a consciousness. That was true in the private counseling. It was also true of the worship service that consciously held the matter of confession and forgiveness before the individual — be he the pastor or the parishioner. These seemed to make a greater impact of change than those which did not. There is nothing to indicate that a classroom can be a substitute for the instrumentation just because it is a classroom. Rather, a prime factor in anything being an effective instrument is the awareness of the individual of the *need* for receiving forgiveness and the *means* of receiving it. After taking the test, one college student seemed to reflect the thoughts of many when she wrote:

The confessing and forgiving experience is a real part of my life experience. This process is very real to me as it helps me to adjust to everyday affairs. Confession, I feel, is a part of prayer where one opens up one's *whole* heart completely revealing the most painful sins to God. To release oneself from the burden of guilt frees one to let loose one's potential.

Note the reference to freedom as well as the lifting of one's burden. The student concluded:

The forgiving experience is not as easy to realize in its fullest extent. . . . One must have faith to accept this gift of forgiveness . . . ; but to have this faith is a gift from God and is something that grows inside and lets one free to forgive others. I feel that forgiveness is felt when one can *forgive* and forget others' sins against oneself.

This concluding statement mentions not only freedom from something in the past but freedom to something in the future. It goes on to identify the experience of being forgiven with the experience of being able to forgive others.

These quotes are not to indicate that everyone must think of forgiveness as does she. They are to indicate that when one does find an adequate instrumentation of forgiveness, it has a genuine liberating and creative effect. It allows a person a sense of freedom with regard to the chains of the past. It also allows freedom to be creative in regard to relationships of the future. In evangelistic preaching, forgiveness is often identified only with the matters of the past. Dynamically, experience from pastoral care indicates that forgiveness must also be identified with experience of the future if it is to be " realized forgiveness."

The final area of testing is that of the shift-of-feeling, or forgiveness scale, chart. This chart was given to five different people for use in control situations. In the chart the total possible score is 64. The scores of five control tests — four taken over a period of two hours and one taken over a period of a day — were as follows: 35 became 28, 45 remained 45, 38 became 31, 45 remained 45, and 59 became 49. This last score was for the test that represented the full day at work in New York.

Two points are of particular relevance here. The first is the obvious one that in each control situation the feeling of being forgiven either remained unchanged or dropped. The second is that within each test, there were shifts. The total score may have remained the same. Yet, because one category was rated more highly and another rated more lowly, the pattern within the test was not the same. In these shifts, it is interesting to note that, in every instance, the category " I feel a sense of freedom " dropped.

In five other instances, the shift-of-feeling chart was used in connection with a worship service in which I was the preacher and in which the liturgy was arranged with both the backward and forward look of forgiveness in mind. After the call to worship, the invocation, and the first hymn, there was a period of silent confession. At this place the congregation was pointedly invited to confess to God not only any sin but also any sense of need for God. After the silence, a statement was given that reminded the people of God's assurance of pardon. From that point, the service moved to the reading of the Scripture, the pastoral prayer, and the sermon. After the sermon, the period of the offering was used to give occasion for a positive confession of faith. This was done pointedly through such expressions as, " Let us confess our forgiveness of each other through the act of our offering " or, " As before we confessed our distance from God, let us now confess our awareness of God's closeness to us." This was then followed by the offering and the prayer of dedication. It should further be observed that the sermon for that particular day was an exposition of the miracle wherein Jesus healed the man lowered through the roof on a stretcher.

Each of these test scores showed a rise. The scores changed in the following way: 43 became 47, 44 became 46, 53 became 60, 49 became 52, and 52 became 53. In some instances the rise was slight, and in some instances it was decided. In each instance, however, the major shift was in a sense of freedom. Almost always this category moved up more than one point. Next to it in degree of shift came the ability to accept people and the ability to forgive people.

Of further interest was the fact that whereas the three items mentioned invariably moved up — and never moved downward — the category " I am the kind of person whom people can accept " often dropped. The category " People forgive me " did not usually drop, but it was the most apt to remain stationary or move up only slightly. On the surface this runs counter to the generally accepted theory that the atmosphere of the counseling room must be an accepting atmosphere if one is to grow and be able to accept others. It seems a reversal of the text, " We love because God first loved us."

A further look, however, suggests that this category of non-acceptance by other people, and the use made of it by those taking the test, is a reflection of the difference between the context and the instrumentality of forgiveness. This test does not ask what it was that made it possible for the people to shift the scores as they did. Dynamically, acceptance by other people may (and I am sure does) have a fundamental role in mediating the forgiveness. As a part of the context, the point of view of psychotherapy is correct.

This device, however, asks how people feel about the realities of the situation at a given moment. In asking one person about the drop in that category (people's acceptance), he replied: " Oh, I don't mean you or my close friends. I mean that I am coming to see that it *is* difficult for many people to accept me. To them, as long as I have an accent, I am a foreigner; and they find it hard to accept my ways and approach." Thus, the drop in this category was commensurate with the rise in the category of freedom.

For this individual had become freer to look at and not be threatened by the effect he had on others. By any standards, increased ability to see reality is growth.

In one instance, it was possible to have a parishioner mark the shift-of-feeling sheet in relation to a counseling hour and then in relation to a church service. In both cases, I was the pastor. Hence, the major difference was in her attitudes and feelings not only in relation to the two types of situations but also in relation to me in two different roles. The exciting part about research is its unpredictability. Whenever it looks as though something is sure, something else emerges to confound the issue. After the counseling hour, the score did not increase, it dropped — 35 became 34.

This unexpected change would be more unsettling were it not for the fact that the interview released a number of thoughts that were new and somewhat disturbing to the parishioner. Hence, until these could be more adequately dealt with, one would not expect a full sense of forgiveness in its various expressions. A look at the test showed an increase in the category " I am liked " and in the category concerning freedom. The drop came in those points which concerned being able to forgive, being the type of person people can accept, and in being forgiven.

Thus, this particular test would indicate that freedom may be an evidence of forgiveness, but it is not to be equated with forgiveness. Rather, again freedom seems to have to do with the context of forgiveness wherein the parishioner was made able to look at things. Toward the end of the interview, she observed that she was the type of person whom people could like on the outside. " But if they knew what I was really like, they would not accept me." This differentiation was reflected in the shifts of the test.

This further indicates, then, that the full realization of forgiveness involves more than just the contextual dimension. Until she could find the instrument that would allow her to make that forgiveness real in all dimensions of her life, it would not be real.

Much to my surprise the same test with the same person, given before and after the service of worship, showed a decidedly different pattern. The score moved from 37 to 43. Again, internally there was a move up in the matter of freedom; but this time, there was also an increase in the categories " I am forgiven," " God loves me," and " I can accept people as they are." When I asked the parishioner to describe what had happened to make such a difference, she began by saying that it was not just the sermon. (Obviously the difficulty with preaching the priesthood of all believers and asking people to express themselves is that they often do.) She said that she listened to the sermon, but that it was the whole service, of which the sermon was a part, that was important to her.

This is further evidence that the instrumentation depends upon the person, the particular instrument, and the particular situation. This test and interview would indicate that an instrument is necessary, that a worship service can be such an instrument, and that when related to an hour of counseling (only twenty-four hours separated the two), it can be tremendously valuable.

To what has been presented above, there is the documentation of the shift-of-feeling test taken by four persons who were Roman Catholic. In the tests taken by these four, much of what has been said above received further confirmation. " Freedom " again proved to be the most volatile of the categories. The shifts on overall scores were greater than in some of the Protestant scores, and about the same as some others. The four laymen and laywomen showed the following changes for the experience of confession: 35 became 56 and 43 became 48. In the matter of the worship service, one had a shift of change from 37 to 59, and for one person 48 remained 48. A Roman Catholic priest also checked the shift-of-feeling sheet. The prime difference between him and the parishioners was that he showed his ultimately highest score in the experience of the worship service instead of the experience of the confession. This is not surprising because, as a priest, his understanding of the instrumentality of the Mass would be higher than that of most laymen. His shift of score for confession was from 37 to 57. His shift in the experience of worship was from 42 to 58.

This set of tests not only gives emphasis to points that have been made above but also heightens the place and value of individual confrontation as an instrument of making forgiveness real. It further suggests that in making forgiveness real, the combination of worship and personal confrontation can be tremendously helpful.

V   EXPANSION OF THE SHIFT-OF-FEELING TEST

After the previous tests had been completed and the research on the following chapters had been done, several questions arose. What would happen if the phrases that grew out of the Bible and the Reformation period were also added to the shift-of-feeling test? As will be seen in the next chapters, the experience of forgiveness is sometimes identified with the experience of lifting a weight and with a sense of strength as well as of freedom. Where do these experiences fit in the modern world? Further, what would happen if this test was applied to a larger group than the one I had worked with in my parish area? Would further exploration confirm or deny what has already been said? Finally, is this whole concept of " realized forgiveness " something that is genuinely relevant to the layman, or is it just part of theological gymnastics?

Frankly, not all these questions can be answered; but considerable light is shed on them, thanks to the cooperation of those who attended a young adult conference held on Labor Day Weekend, 1963, on the New Jersey shore. There, over one hundred men and women, ages seventeen to forty, gathered for a weekend. This was not a highly confined retreat. The conferees had time to swim, boat, play ball, and take short trips to a nearby amusement center. There were a few married couples. Although the denominational makeup was predominately Presbyterian, the group also had Methodists, Lutherans, and a few Congregationalists and Episcopalians.

The theme of the conference was " The Christian Personality." On Friday night, I presented the testing materials and the main idea of the conference. As the speaker for the weekend, I gave a lecture Saturday morning and Saturday afternoon on " Personality Development " and " The Dynamics of Forgiveness," respectively. Each of these lectures was followed by a period for small-group discussion. The discussions lasted a minimum of forty-five minutes. Each group numbered six to eight people, plus a leader. The leaders were volunteers who had had a two-hour training period under the direction of Rev. Ernest Bartow — a young minister who served as adviser to the program. Mr. Bartow presented an up-to-date concept of group dynamics and taught primarily by the use of role-playing.

After the lecture-discussion periods, Saturday evening was given over to cabin skits and recreation. Sunday centered on a worship service, conducted by Mr. Bartow; an afternoon discussion of the church in foreign lands, led by a sociologist; recreation; an evening question-and-answer period with me; and a presentation of a summer work-camp project in Bolivia. On Monday, after a business meeting and lunch, the conference closed with the service of Holy Communion.

It must be clear that the place of forgiveness as an experience was consciously in our minds as we planned the conference. There was no attempt or desire to aggravate a sense of guilt or to create a false one. The entire approach was that of trying to meet people where they were.

For the purposes of testing, two categories were added to the shift-of-feeling test: "I feel a sense of strength" and "I feel a weight lifted." [20] The test was placed on different colors of paper. Those who received blue sheets were instructed to take the test before and after the entire conference. Their tests would indicate what happened in the total experience of the conference. Those who received yellow sheets were asked to take the test before and after the Sunday worship service when Mr. Bartow spoke of forgiveness on the basis of the parable about the prodigal son. Pink sheets were used by those who took the test before and after one of the lecture-discussion periods (i.e., the total hour and a half that included the talk and the small-group discussion). The test was also given to a group who took it before and after a period of recreation. These people, I hoped, would show if walking one's dog, playing a game of golf, or going to a ball game was as effective as going to church! They took the test on green sheets. By testing reactions to the recreation periods, lecture-discussions, and worship service, as well as to the total conference, I hoped that I would find a basis for comparing different types of experience.

The reaction of the young adults was interesting to me from my standpoint as a leader in the conference. Initially, there was keen interest in what was being done. After the first of the small-group discussions, however, it was clear that some were confused, others upset, and still others resentful. After giving the afternoon talk and listening to the results of some of the small-group discussions, I was discouraged. The few ministers present seemed to understand and even to be enthusiastic about the presentations. Yet, for myself I had the feeling that I simply had not communicated to the group as a whole. The rest of the afternoon was marked by a number of discussions. Some dealt with personal problems. Others consisted of probing questions about my presentations. All these discussions showed how legalistically most of us think about life, in general, and faith, in particular.

The breakthrough came that night. It was provided by the delegates themselves. Each cabin was to present a skit. Those of us who were leaders were asked to judge. One of the skits from a cabin of men was a takeoff on a small-group discussion. It was cleverly done. The great point of controversy was whether or not forgiveness could help the New York Mets baseball team. After the nature of the Gridiron Club dinners, the skit provided hard-hitting and good-natured spoofing. Not only was the skit entertaining but the laughter allowed a marvelous release of tension, hostility, and embarrassment. The fact that we picked this skit for first place symbolized everyone's acceptance of this release and recognized the ability shown in the skit.

As a result, the feeling of the group on Sunday seemed much different from the feeling on Saturday. The skit itself showed that more had been communicated than I realized; otherwise it could not have been done. The worship experience became an opportunity consciously to share in what we had been talking about. That night, the question-and-answer period allowed for clarification of feelings, insights, and understandings. Defensiveness seemed to disappear almost entirely, and there was a marked upsurge of informal discussions, desire for personal counseling, and expressions of excitement over new personal discoveries.

I am not really able to discuss the significance of the service of Communion. I was too subjectively involved in it. There was place in the service for positive and negative confession, for the instrumentation of both, and for examples of that which is discussed in these pages. All I can really say is that for me it was a " mountaintop experience "; and it seems to have been such for others too. The meaningfulness of the Sacrament as an expression of the real presence of Christ and the meaningfulness of the worshiping group as the church of which I was a part were very strong. I would find it difficult to analyze this further.

What, then, of the tests? Of the ninety test sheets distributed, fifty-four were returned. Four of these were incomplete and therefore discarded. Seven were returned from the recreation group. Of these, one showed a downward shift of minus one. The highest shift upward was eleven. The average shift of feeling was a positive or plus shift of three and five tenths. In other words, to that degree, after a period of recreation, people changed their marks to indicate a greater sense of feeling forgiven.

Thirteen tests were returned from the group who took them in connection with the lecture-discussion periods. Although the overall average shift was greater than that of the recreation group, perhaps the main factor was the *degree* of shift registered by some people. Whereas most of the recreation group showed shifts of two or three points, with the one exception, the lecture-discussion group had one shift of minus one, three of three, two of four, two of five, one of seven, one of sixteen, and one of eighteen. The average shift was a positive one of five points increase. This is a definite and consistent difference when compared with the group involved in recreation. As a means of feeling forgiven, golf loses out!

The results of the tests taken in connection with the service of worship are in the same direction as those of the lecture-discussion group, but even more pronounced. The average shift is upward of five and nine tenths points. That is a higher average change than seen in either the discussion or recreation group. Even more significant, however, is the wide variation of scores. The lowest shift was minus six and the highest twenty-four. Of the fourteen who took the test, four registered a drop in that which would indicate a feeling of " realized forgiveness." Two of these dropped only one point, but one was minus four and another minus six. This does not say that something was wrong with the service of worship. It does say that out of such a service one may not complete the move from guilt to forgiveness and may come away at some midpoint in the process.

The positive shifts show a striking contrast to those of the other two groups. Whereas the lecture-discussion group had several shifts of seven or more, the worship group had only four shifts of less than ten (not counting the negative scores). There were two at ten, two at eleven, one at fourteen, and one at twenty-four.

Interesting as these are, the most striking results come in the scores of those who took the tests before and after the conference. The average shift of this group was almost double the shift of the worship group or the lecture-discussion group. The average shift of the sixteen tests was nine and eight tenths. Three of these were negative: two at minus five and one at minus one. Of the positive group, only four were less than ten. Unlike the worship group, only one of these four is less than six. The rest of the scores indicate a positive shift of two at eleven, one at twelve, one each at fifteen, sixteen, twenty-one, twenty-four, and thirty.

What do these results mean? At the outset they indicate, again, the fact that there are various situations in which a person can have a meaningful experience. Further, these tests confirm the point already made about the fact that something can happen in a worship service. In the framework of the conference, the worship service was the single most effective means of experiencing an increase on those points which pertain to awareness of forgiveness.

Above all, however, a comparison of the tests shows the value of a combined set of experiences. It is no surprise to anyone that more can happen at a weekend retreat than in one hour on Sunday morning. What may be a surprise is the degree of difference. In addition, the results of the test taken by those who reflect the experience of the entire weekend underscore a previous observation, viz., worship by itself may be meaningful, but not nearly as significant as when combined with another "means of grace." Previously I mentioned the place it has when combined with the experience of confession. Here, the value of worship is seen when combined with a form of education as well as opportunities for confession.

A derivative suggestion from these tests is that the initial size of a group does not matter. It is what is done within the group to give people intimate experiences of relationship that counts. The total attendance could have been twenty or two hundred, instead of one hundred. By dividing the larger group into small subgroups, however, everyone had an opportunity to experience what was necessary for making the large worship service of value. This would suggest that whether or not a church is small or large does not make an ultimate difference. What makes the difference is the opportunity, within the large group, to find a small fellowship in which personal interaction can take place.

These tests also indicate something about the relevance of the Biblical description of forgiveness for the present day. As in other tests, the categories of freedom and acceptance showed definite action. On the tests taken after participation in the recreation, the worship, and the lecture-discussion groups, the categories " lifting a weight " and " a sense of strength " showed almost no change at all. The lack of shifts in these two items seemed to indicate that they were not relevant to modern people. Yet, in private discussion I often found that people were using these phrases as new ways of expressing what they did or did not feel. It is pertinent, therefore, to note that in the test group that reflected the whole conference these two items did show considerable motion.

Hence, although it still is not clear how much the Biblical usages mean in current ways of talking, it surely is true that they are relevant for some people. The tests also confirm that people do not often speak in terms of " forgiveness" or lack of it, but they talk much of those experiences which are identified with the meaning of forgiveness. This is seen in the fact that the items that used the word " forgiveness " seldom moved as much as the items that expressed some aspect of personal life.

From a testing standpoint, what has been said about the conference is only hypothetical. Questions could be raised that can be answered only by more precise instruments than the shift-of-feeling chart. Nevertheless, if the correlation between this instrument and the Q-sort test has any basis, these results are further evidence (1) of the experience of " realized forgiveness " as an important and central part of personal growth and (2) of the positive relationship that is possible between worship, education, and counseling or confession, on one hand, and forgiveness on the other.

VI CONCLUSION

Again it must be emphasized that the preceding research in no way proves the points that have been made. It does indicate, however, that from the experience of the parish, there are certain working hypotheses that are legitimate.

From the foregoing, it is necessary to hold that forgiveness is not simply a synonym for words like acceptance, freedom, release, or even atonement. Rather, forgiveness makes it possible to accept and to atone. Freedom is partly expressed through forgiveness and also helps mediate forgiveness.

Forgiveness is not to be understood in any other than dynamic terms.[21] To do so is to describe something other than what happens to an individual when he realizes forgiveness in his own life. " Realized forgiveness " is a dynamic that can be known not directly but by its results. One dimension of this dynamic is a context that allows one to be free. This freedom may be expressed as freedom from guilt, freedom to love, or freedom just to wait and see what must be done. Any way it is expressed, it is freedom.

The other dimension of this dynamic is an instrumentality. How is the forgiveness and the freedom to create going to be expressed? That is the problem of instrumentality. For Gandhi, this was not expressed by the church because of his experience in England when a parish insulted him. For Mr. Sim, it was not expressed by his particular parish because he could not give expression to the context of his freedom. He could do it only in AA. However, the expression and the instrumentation of forgiveness can be in confession, in worship, in a cell group, in preaching, or in the Sacrament. This is to say that when the dynamics of forgiveness are taken seriously, the so-called " means of grace " literally become *means* of grace. Otherwise they are just forms.

Where does Christ relate to this picture? Whether one is speaking of Sigmund Freud and psychoanalysis, Carl Rogers and clinical psychology, or Talcott Parsons and sociological research, one underlying assumption is held: estrangement in part is estrangement in all. Translated, this means that a person who is not at peace with himself or his fellowman is not at peace with God. A person who is at one with God is at one with those about him and with himself. The same thought is expressed theologically when it is observed that it is impossible to separate the love of God and the love of man. Therefore, insofar as one is bound and has not come to terms with the heart of man, one has not come to terms with the heart of the universe. In the Christian faith, Jesus is the one in whom the relation both to the universe and to man becomes unified. Thus, from the modern pastorate, we now turn to the Scripture and the early church to understand not only their views of forgiveness but the way in which they understood Jesus to relate to the realization of forgiveness.

This transition is made in the belief that the irrelevance of the church in the modern day is the failure of the church to understand the reality of forgiveness. As a living experience, forgiveness is needed and is relevant to the condition of man. Without it, man cannot live. Without it, he cannot grow. In thought, people of the church may shift from this to that theology. In worship, people of the church may shift from this to that form. However, these shifts are quite unimportant if they do not begin with an awareness of dynamics of "realized forgiveness." Dietrich Bonhoeffer spoke of the need for obedience to Christ as central in the Christian faith. Obedience is important but not central. Obedience to Christ is important because what is central is the realization of forgiveness that comes through him.

Pastor Bonhoeffer wrote that the cost of discipleship is obedience. It is not. In fact, obedience can be what he aptly called "cheap grace." The real cost of discipleship is to accept forgiveness — and that is a genuine sacrifice. It means that a man must surrender his god-centeredness about himself, his ego, his all to the true God. The obedience is not to words by which we denote salvation. The obedience is to the reception of forgiveness in Him who incarnates forgiveness; and man's obedience compels him to find the words, i.e., the instruments that will allow that forgiveness to become real. People want to be saved in the present day as in Biblical days. The only difference is the language people use.

That the realization of forgiveness is central to the Scripture, and that the picture of forgiveness that emerges from the parish has its counterpart in the Scripture, is the message of the next chapter.

3

The Bible and the
Dynamics of Forgiveness

I METHOD IN BIBLE-READING

ONE may listen to different individuals, or read different parts of the Bible, or look at different periods of history. No matter which of these a person does, one fact will become obvious, viz., that every generation will find its own meaning for the word " forgiveness." In one period, "forgiveness" may be understood as "salvation." To another generation, it may mean "peace." The absence of fear may be paramount in the understanding of forgiveness in the parishioner who speaks with the minister at nine o'clock; at eleven, another parishioner may speak of forgiveness in terms of life as opposed to death.

The same differences are found in the Bible. The Hebrew word that is most often translated " forgiveness " means " to have a weight lifted." Yet, the Biblical experience most often described as related to forgiveness is strength. In the Bible as well as in the pastoral interviews, these different interpretations reflect different expressions of another dimension of forgiveness: the freedom to be newly creative.

However, these statements presuppose agreement on how the Bible is to be read. What was said in the previous chapter about the approach to theology must now be applied to the Bible itself. Therefore, the first question is, " How do we read the Bible? "

The reaction of some right-wing magazines to my study on remarriage makes it obvious that the " how " of Bible study is crucial. Most conservative magazines were favorable to the overall method in that study but asked for clarification about how I approached the Scripture. Such honest appraisal is helpful and appreciated.[1]

Let there be no lack of clarity about my approach. In what follows, there is an underlying assumption about the Bible. It is an assumption that the Bible is something other than just a collection of events. Rather, the Bible is an expression of the experience of the church. It is an expression of the church in two ways. In one way, individuals of the church picked different experiences and put them together to identify what they considered the important and true revelation of God. This is seen particularly in the Gospel writers. No one of them wrote a history. Each picked from his various sources of information that which he felt would show forth God's act in history and in Christ.

The second way in which the Bible expresses the experience of the church is through the formation of the Bible itself. There were many writings and many gospel accounts that could have been used. The church chose only sixty-six books because it was felt that these books expressed the true revelation of God. The fact that the church chose these books is another way of saying that the Bible is an expression of the faith of the church as to what God has revealed.[2]

If it is true that the forming of the Bible is an expression of the faith of the church, that fact gives the first basis for reading the Bible. " Realized forgiveness " is at the heart of the Scripture. Indeed, it is inconceivable that the Bible could have been written apart from the experience of the forgiveness of God. By the same token, the Bible cannot be understood apart from the realization of the forgiveness of God. Studying the Bible may help one become aware of God's forgiveness, but without the context of that forgiveness which makes the person free to see what he reads, reading even the Bible is impossible.

In one sense, then, the present chapter is a pre-patristic study of church history. This is not just a chapter on the Bible after which we will move to several chapters on sections of church history. This chapter is itself a chapter on the history of the church's first experience of the realization of forgiveness. In another sense, though, this chapter is also post-patristic. It is not a chapter that tells how to be forgiven by reading the Bible. *This* chapter is a section on how reading the Bible becomes meaningful when a person has experienced the forgiveness that the early church felt.

To say that forgiveness makes Bible-reading possible is to say that forgiveness brings a certain perspective to the Scripture and raises certain questions of the writings.

A. *Consider the matter of perspective first*.[3] Specifically to capture what the Bible says about "realized forgiveness," the reader must recognize that the term belongs peculiarly to pastoral theology. Without recognition of this point, the method for a proper understanding of forgiveness in the Bible is lost. (For elaboration of this point, attention is called to the notes.) [4]

The research in pastoral work shows that there is a contextual and an instrumental dimension to the realization of forgiveness. This view is required not only by the research but, when looking at the comparable experience in the Bible, by the Scripture as well. This distinction between forgiveness as a context and forgiveness as an instrument is generally missed in Biblical study itself. It is missed either in not recognizing the difference or in identifying one pole with the other. Both *The Interpreter's Dictionary of the Bible* and the discussion by Rudolf Bultmann are cases in point.

The article on forgiveness in *The Interpreter's Dictionary of the Bible* states that Jesus, " by his stress on the necessity of a forgiving spirit, . . . insists that repentance go beyond sorrow for sin and issue in a radical reorientation of personality." [5] Undoubtedly, forgiveness involves the reorientation of personality. That change, however, is not all that there is to forgiveness. Rather, the reorientation is one of the ways in which forgiveness becomes real. To speak of what actualizes forgiveness is to speak of forgiveness as an instrument. *The Interpreter's Dictionary of the Bible* article says that man must have a " forgiving spirit." But what makes it possible to forgive others? Those who point to the statement in Matthew that commands forgiveness forget that Jesus could give his command because everyone who heard it was standing in his presence. Christ could command our forgiveness of others because God's forgiveness showed through Jesus Christ himself. He was the context that made the instrument possible. Thus, when the article in *The Interpreter's Dictionary of the Bible* insists that the central element in Jesus' teaching about forgiveness is the need to forgive others, it is reducing forgiveness to an instrument or confusing the instrument with the context. The article makes it appear as though forgiving others were the context in which forgiveness could become real. Actually, it is the other way around.

Similarly, Bultmann states that the demand to love and to forgive one's neighbor has this effect: it puts a person in a relation to his neighbor whereby he sets aside all rights and faces the judgment of God alone.[6] He says that forgiving puts others out of the picture of judgment, and we stand in that judgment by ourselves. This, again, is dealing with forgiveness as just an instrument, for it identifies forgiveness with an act. Dynamically, the experience of being forgiven can be a threatening experience, for it means admitting that we are not all-sufficient. It means admitting that we are not God, and it means admitting that we need the grace of God. To that point, Bultmann is surely correct. To say that forgiveness is threatening, however, is to say that the nature of God's judgment is forgiveness. It is his very forgiveness that judges us. From the standpoint of the previous chapter, and from the standpoint of the method by which forgiveness must be approached, Bultmann's overall statement is wrong. It is not the forgiving of other people that then makes it possible to experience the judgment of God and to receive of his forgiveness. Rather, it is the context of the forgiveness of God that judges us and thereby frees us for making that forgiveness real in our attitude toward other people.

The error of both *The Interpreter's Dictionary of the Bible* and of Bultmann is that they have approached "forgiveness" as a purely Biblical word. As a result, they have treated forgiveness in terms of one question and one meaning when, in reality, forgiveness must be treated in terms of two questions and two meanings.

The distinction between forgiveness as an instrument and forgiveness as a context is also missed by all views that identify the unforgivable sin against the Holy Spirit as an *act*. Jesus said that every sin would be forgiven except the sin against the Holy Spirit. Periodically, people come to the church afraid that they have committed the sin against the Holy Spirit. In the terms of this book, however, any act is part of the instrumental in forgiveness. A person may not have forgiven his neighbor. That is a sin, but it is not the unforgivable sin, because one can always begin forgiving his neighbor. The forgiving acts are the instruments by which forgiveness becomes real.

The sin that is unforgivable is the rejection of forgiveness as a context. It is the rejection of that dynamic power of the Holy Spirit which, through the context of forgiveness, frees us. The thieves on the cross and the story of Job are two Biblical demonstrations of the difference between forgiveness as a context and as an instrument.

Both thieves were within the context of the forgiving Christ. The one thief cursed God and, in so doing, rejected the context of forgiveness. If the swearing had been just an act of temper, poor taste, or weakness, such as Peter denying his Lord, the consequences would not need to have been more serious for the thief than they were for Peter. Instead, his words were a rejection of the very context of forgiveness. This point the other thief quickly caught when he said, "Do you not fear God. . . ?" The other thief did not reject the context of forgiveness.

The story of Job can be described as the struggle of a man, not to reject the context of forgiveness, but to find the instrumentation that would make the context real. Even his wife said, "Curse God, and die." That is to say, she suggested that he follow the way of the first thief. Job would not.

Two events provided the instrumentation that made God real. The first was when Job became aware of arguing with God himself. On the surface, it looks as though God is scolding Job when he says, "Who is this that darkens counsel by words without knowledge?" On the contrary, the fact of the confrontation made the context real. It is not Job's arguing that God rejects. Instead, when Job seems to stop the argument and not wrestle with God, God says, "Gird up your loins like a man; I will question you, and you declare to me" (Job 40:7). God is saying, "Do not abandon the context."

The second event was Job's repentance and prayer for others. The repentance is expressed at the end of the poem. Aware of the context of forgiveness: "Now my eye sees thee," Job makes it real through the instrumentation of repentance: "Therefore I despise myself, and repent in dust and ashes" (Job 42:5-6). The prayer for others is expressed in the concluding narrative. In Job 42:8, God says that he will hear the prayer of Job for his friends "not to deal with you according to your folly."

As in the instances of parish care, none of this says that these people were conscious of the workings of forgiveness as they did these things. It does say that the method of seeing life in terms of a dynamic field gives a valid basis for perceiving two dimensions that repeatedly appear to be a part of the experience of forgiveness as a personal reality.

This failure to see the two dimensions of forgiveness can also be found in the Bible itself. In the sweep of the Bible, I believe a case can be made for the statement that wherever this error occurred, there was need for a reformation. Whenever the priests sought to identify the context of forgiveness with the instrumentation of forgiveness, there was trouble. Temple ritual was the instrumentation. Every time that that ritual was made the basis of salvation, the priests were identifying the context with the instrumentation. Thus, after the exodus the people, under Aaron, built a golden calf. The giving of the law on the part of Moses was a reformation. In the late seventh century B.C., under Josiah, when church worship as well as community life had reached a low ebb, the book of Deuteronomy came forth with another reformation of the times. Supremely, under Christ, the Pharisees and scribes had confused the instrumentation of forgiveness through the ritual law with the context. Therefore, Jesus had to reform the procedure with his dictum that the Sabbath was made for man and not man for the Sabbath. Wherever, in the Scripture, people forgot the basis for understanding forgiveness that is mentioned here, reformation came.[7]

Someone may protest that the idea of a context and an instrumentation of the context grows out of personality research and not out of the Bible. It is true that the analogy of field theory, from which the idea of context and instrument developed, does not originate with the Bible. Yet, in order to understand the experiences of Biblical life and the Biblical view of time, the field analogy is required. (In order not to lose sight of the purpose of this chapter, I enlarge on this point in the notes rather than here.) [8]

Basically, the Bible can be understood rigidly and legalistically, or dynamically and experientially. The former leads only to contradictions and inconsistencies. The latter alone is true to the Christian interpretation. To ignore this will lead to an irrelevant view of forgiveness. It is precisely because forgiveness has not been understood in this light that its relevancy to the Christian faith and the relevancy of the Christian faith to man's needs have been *missed*.

B. From the discussion of perspective, *we move to the questions which that perspective brings to the Bible*. In this study, the word "forgiveness" is to be understood from the standpoint of an experience realized in peoples' lives. From what the previous chapter told of this experience, what then are the questions that are asked of the Bible which will determine the definition of "forgiveness"?

There are two initial questions. First, "What did the person who wrote believe about forgiveness?" Second, "What did his situation or experience reveal about forgiveness as he experienced it?" These two are not necessarily the same. Often, a person's description of forgiveness does not describe what actually happened to him. Further, it is usually found that what a person says generally separates the two aspects of "realized forgiveness." What actually happens to a person reveals both dimensions together.

The field analogy warns us about the use of the two basic questions that we are asking. It says that the two questions are related as poles in a field, but that one does not cause the other. If we ask what people mean by the word "forgiveness," we are asking, "What is the means by which this person made real his experience of forgiveness?" We are asking specifically about his instrumentation. When Jesus said that we must forgive if we are to be forgiven, he was saying that the instrument that helps make our own forgiveness real to us is the very act of forgiving others. He was not describing the whole field of experience.

If, however, we ask, "What is the nature of forgiveness as revealed by the person's experience? " regardless of what the person says, we are asking something different. Here, we really are asking, " What is the context in which the instrument works? " We are not asking about the context alone, but how people can be made free and how people do experience forgiveness.

Both questions are important and both poles are necessary. Biblically, without the context the instrument is useless, and without the instrument the context never comes alive. Both are poles or centers of influence within a common field, without either of which the dynamics of forgiveness itself would not exist.

II [9] FORGIVENESS EXPRESSED AS LIFTING A WEIGHT

The basic Old Testament word that is translated " forgiveness " is *shalach*. According to Gesenius, this word has the primary meaning of " lightness, lifting up." [10] The Septuagint, according to Girdlestone, sometimes translates this Hebrew word with the Greek *aphiēmi* — " to remit." [11] Strangely, this basic idea of lifting is missed in many writings on forgiveness, but Biblically it is a central theme.

In the Old Testament, forgiveness does not mean denial of the past. Rather, it comes to mean removal of the effect of the past upon the present. Hence, forgiveness is spoken of as the " Divine restoration of an offender into favour." [12] Again and again, forgiveness is associated with some means of instrumentation. Usually it is some form of talking the problem out. It may be public confession or private. For example, Ps. 130 speaks of crying out or calling. " Deep calls to deep " and in that experience, the forgiveness of God becomes clear at the depths. The Hebrew word for " call " is *cara*, which later comes to mean " preaching " or " proclaiming." Hence, the realization of forgiveness is related to the most basic form of communication and then runs the whole gamut of types of communication.

The relation of the context and the instrumental is pointed out by Girdlestone when he says that the word *shalach* is used only of God to man, never of man to man (thus indicating the context) , and that without the shedding of blood there is no forgiveness (thus indicating that the instrumental nature is necessary) .

There are also other Hebrew words used in the Old Testament

to convey the idea of forgiveness. These may be translated variously as " to cover," " to pardon," and " to wipe away." Again, with each of these the basic sin is not undone, but the effect of the sin is removed. Thus, in the Hebrew word *macha*,[13] the primary meaning is " to stroke " or " to rub over." The root shows that what has been done cannot be undone, but that the purpose of forgiveness is to remove the effect of the sin.

In the Old Testament, the dynamic of forgiveness appears to be that of releasing one from bondage to a past act. Insofar as this is true, the Biblical idea of forgiveness and the psychological idea of acceptance are not synonymous. Forgiveness may make acceptance possible; and acceptance may help portray forgiveness. They are not, however, equivalent. Wherever Scripture uses the word " acceptance," it uses an altogether different root, one that carries the meaning of " receive." In the Scripture, acceptance and forgiveness are not confused.

In the New Testament, insofar as the word is concerned, the Hebrew meaning is carried over. *Aphiēmi,* which was used in the Septuagint to translate *shalach,* is the word used most often to indicate forgiveness. The idea of sending away or remitting continues. The dynamic idea of forgiveness as not being the elimination of what happened is suggested when Jesus says, " Not an iota, not a dot, will pass from the law until all is accomplished." It is the effect of what has happened to man in relation to the structure of the law that shall be removed.

The fact that every use of the word " forgiveness " refers to the removal of the effect of sin means that the particular forgiveness will depend on the nature of the sin or the particular view of that sin. " It [forgiveness] is the act which re-establishes man in his true relationship to God by removing the element which destroys that relationship, namely, sin, man's transgression."[14]

With this word study as background, the basic questions now come to the fore: (1) " What is the nature of forgiveness as a context in which forgiveness as an instrument can work? " (2) " What is the instrument by which a person makes real the experience of forgiveness as a context? " To these two initial questions we also add a third: (3) " What is the nature of the field in which the two polarities of forgiveness operate? "

The contextual nature of forgiveness is seen primarily in the Biblical views of the covenant. In Genesis, God blesses Noah and says, " I establish my covenant with you, that never again shall all flesh be cut off by the waters of a flood, and never again shall there be a flood to destroy the earth " (Gen. 9:11). As a sign of this covenant, God says, " I set my bow in the cloud " (v. 13). In the midst of this context, the Bible then goes on to describe the creativity of Noah and the freedom of Noah. He was creative in that he was a tiller of the soil (v. 20). His freedom was misused, as was Mr. Sim's, in drunkenness; but the very misuse is evidence of his freedom.

Likewise, the contextual nature of forgiveness is described in God's promise to Abraham. God says, " And I will make of you a great nation, and I will bless you, and make your name great, so that you will be a blessing " (Gen. 12:2). The context of this covenant gives Abraham, then called Abram, the freedom to "go forth." Several chapters later, when Abraham questions the promise because he has no heir by his wife, God says: " I am God Almighty; walk before me, and be blameless. And I will make my covenant between me and you, and will multiply you exceedingly " (Gen. 17:1-2). To this, Abraham replies, " Behold, my covenant is with you." Here, the fundamental nature of the dynamics of forgiveness emerges again. Abraham becomes creative — thanks to the context of forgiveness which has about it the nature of a covenant.

Throughout the Old Testament, the constancy and complete reliability of God are the main ingredients in forgiveness as a context. Consider Moses and the Ten Commandments. In the Commandments, the validity of the dynamic approach, as opposed to the legalistic approach, should again be noted. It is not the following of the ten points of the law that makes it possible to be at one with God. Prior to the statement of the law, there is the preface, " I am the Lord your God, who brought you out of the land of Egypt." It is, therefore, the presence and awareness of the real God which make it possible to know and follow the law — not the reverse.

This preface in Ex. 20:2 indicates the constancy of God's covenant, as does its counterpart in Deut. 5:6. The difference between the two is that in Deuteronomy, a paragraph is given to make clear that it is out of the context of the covenant that the law comes. " The Lord our God made a covenant with us in Horeb," reads Deut. 5:2. Both instances, however, center on the fact that it is the Lord who was with the Hebrews in all the long and terrible days of Egypt, in the days of the flight, in the days of gaining freedom from oppression. Here, and at every moment when the Scripture speaks of " the God of Abraham, the God of Isaac, and the God of Jacob," the constancy of God's covenant is emphasized. It is because one can count on the forgiveness of God that one can have the security to be free.

The nature of the covenant is seen again in the idea of the remnant. The two-sided nature of this constancy is suggested in the opening chapters of Isaiah. Says the prophet: " If the Lord of hosts had not left us a few survivors, we should have been like Sodom, and become like Gomorrah." (Isa. 1:9.) Thus the idea of the remnant is suggested; but why?

One reason is that the constancy of God will not tolerate the reduction of forgiveness as a context to forgiveness as an instrument. " What to me is the multitude of your sacrifices? says the Lord; I have had enough of burnt offerings of rams." (Isa. 1:11.) And again: " When you come to appear before me, who requires of you this trampling of my courts? " (Isa. 1:12.) The use of the sacrifices was denying the contextual nature of forgiveness as seen in the covenant. The negative nature of God's constancy is his wrath whereby he will not tolerate these solemn assemblies. Hence: " When you spread forth your hands, I will hide my eyes from you; even though you make many prayers, I will not listen " (Isa. 1:15) . Therefore, his constancy does not mean that Israel can misuse the context of forgiveness.

On the other side, then, a remnant is necessary because God will never withhold the constancy of his forgiveness despite Israel's misuse of forgiveness. " Come now, let us reason together, says the Lord: though your sins are like scarlet, they shall be as white as snow." (Isa. 1:18.) The Lord speaks of his saving remnant when Isaiah says, " So shall my word be that goes forth from my mouth; it shall not return to me empty " (Isa. 55:11) ; and " I will give them an everlasting name which shall not be cut off " (Isa. 56:5) .

Perhaps the supreme expression of the covenantal nature of the context of forgiveness to be found in the Old Testament is the statement in Jeremiah. It reads: " Behold, the days are coming, says the Lord, when I will make a new covenant with the house of Israel and the house of Judah, not like the covenant which I made with their fathers when I took them by the hand to bring them out of the land of Egypt, my covenant which they broke, though I was their husband, says the Lord. But this is the covenant which I will make with the house of Israel after those days, says the Lord: I will put my law within them, and I will write it upon their hearts; and I will be their God, and they shall be my people.

" And no longer shall each man teach his neighbor and each his brother, saying, ' Know the Lord,' for they shall all know me, from the least of them to the greatest, says the Lord; for I will forgive their iniquity, and I will remember their sin no more." (Jer. 31:31-34.) Here, the constancy of the covenant is confirmed, for it is not a new covenant that is being given. It is the old covenant given in a new way. Here, the relationship between covenant and forgiveness is reiterated because the concept of covenant and forgiveness are placed together. Here, the dynamic and freeing nature of the covenant is seen, for the experience of the forgiven man is realized in his freedom to " know the Lord."

In the close of the Old Testament era, the book of Nehemiah shows by its very construction that the covenant is the context of God's forgiving grace. There, the context of God's covenant was made clear through the children of Israel's being brought out from the exile. It was following that, that the law was read (Neh. 8:8) . Upon the reading of the law, the people then confessed, and gave expression to the forgiveness, for the people began to mourn when they heard the words of the law. However, upon the basis of the explanation given them by the prophet, they went out to celebrate the reality of God's presence. " And all the people went their way to eat and drink and to send portions and to make great rejoicing, because they had understood the words that were declared to them." (Neh. 8:12.) Again, it was the context of God's forgiveness that made the law meaningful.

In the New Testament, the contextual nature of forgiveness is also carried out with the fundamental idea of covenant. The New Testament is itself the New Covenant. Thus, in the institution of the Lord's Supper, as expressed by Paul, Jesus is recorded as saying, " This cup is the new covenant in my blood " (I Cor. 11:25). And one is to come to the Lord's table " discerning the [Lord's] body," for therein is the context that enables us to be judged and to be free from condemnation. For " when we are judged by the Lord, we are chastened so that we may not be condemned along with the world." (I Cor. 11:32.)

Throughout the Bible, we learn something of the nature of the contextual dimension of forgiveness: viz., it is a mediated context. In the Old Testament, the mediation is largely by a corporate group. Israel is a chosen people. In the history of Israel, the significance of this mediation has different interpretations. At one point, the mediation is seen in the very provincial sense of God being the private property of the Israelites. At other points, especially in the book of Jonah, the missionary aspect of this mediation comes forward. Nevertheless, throughout Biblical history, the forgiveness is seen to be mediated.

In the New Testament, and particularly in the epistles, the mediation is not so much by a group as by a person — Jesus Christ. There is a foretaste of the personal mediation of the context of forgiveness in the Old Testament. The familiar Suffering Servant passages of Isaiah speak of one with whose stripes we are healed (Isa. 53:5) and Jeremiah gives promise of a " righteous Branch " which will come forth from David (Jer. 33:15). Yet it is not until the New Testament that the personal mediation of the context of forgiveness reaches its zenith. In his pastoral letter to the disturbed church at Corinth, Paul writes, " If Christ has not been raised, your faith is futile and you are still in your sins " (I Cor. 15:17). In the same chapter he goes on to say, " For as in Adam all die, so also in Christ shall all be made alive " (v. 22). Peter also makes the point that the prophets who prophesied of the grace of God " inquired what person or time was indicated " (I Peter 1:11). In making the same observation, John adds in his epistle, " In this the love of God was made manifest among us, that God sent his only Son into the world " (I John 4:9). The context of God's covenant of forgiveness is mediated through a person. At this point, it is well to note the relationship between Christ as the mediator and the commands Christ gave — especially the command to forgive. Christ could give that command (as said earlier) because he himself was the embodiment of forgiveness. Jesus did not give forgiveness as a law to be added to the religious laws or even to the Ten Commandments. Rather, he commanded what becomes possible when one is truly in the context that he himself provides.

From the individual, the New Testament then returns to an understanding of the mediation of the context of forgiveness through the corporate group.[15] The mediation of the context of forgiveness through the group is suggested primarily in the Gospels and in The Acts. Matthew 16:19, and its counterparts in the other Gospels, presents this corporate mediation when Jesus says, " Whatever you bind on earth shall be bound in heaven, and whatever you loose on earth shall be loosed in heaven." The dramatic demonstration of this promise is put forth in Acts, ch. 5, when Ananias and his wife Sapphira hold back a portion of their goods from the church. This betrayal of the church is seen as betrayal of the context of forgiveness. Peter said, " You have not lied to men but to God " (Acts 5:4) ; and when he heard those words, Ananias died. Of Sapphira, Peter asked, " How is it that you have agreed together to tempt the Spirit of the Lord? " (Acts 5:9) and Sapphira also fell down and died. Whether seen personally or corporately, the context of forgiveness in the Scripture is understood as a mediated context.

Particularly in the New Testament, the context of forgiveness is seen not only as a covenant, and a mediated covenant, but also as a proclaimed covenant. Thus, when the scribes came forward and accused Jesus of being possessed by Beelzebub, he proclaimed to them the context of forgiveness and the danger of rejecting that context. Mark 3:28-29 reads, " Truly, I say to you, all sins will be forgiven the sons of men, and whatever blasphemies they utter; but whoever blasphemes against the Holy Spirit never has forgiveness, but is guilty of an eternal sin." Paul goes on to say,

" Everyone who calls upon the name of the Lord will be saved "
(Rom. 10:13). In that verse, he is speaking of the mediated
context of forgiveness. Paul then proceeds to emphasize the proclaimed nature of the context when he says: " But how are men
to call upon him in whom they have not believed? And how are
they to believe in him of whom they have never heard? And how
are they to hear without a preacher? " (Rom. 10:14).

The contextual nature of forgiveness may also be described as
the Kingdom of God at hand. Forgiveness is something real and
present. It is not something distant and transcendent. Said John
the Baptist, " Repent, for the kingdom of heaven is at hand."
And in the first chapter of Mark, the Baptist united repentance
and forgiveness of sins in a single experience that had its focus in
Christ. Why? Because in Christ the Kingdom of God, the context
of forgiveness, is present.

The presence of this Kingdom is argued even by Jesus. The
Kingdom of Heaven is " within you." " He who has seen me has
seen the Father." (John 14:9.) " Whoever does not receive the
kingdom of God like a child shall not enter it," and then Jesus
put the little child in the midst of the people. As has been previously observed, Jesus asserted that one must forgive others if
he himself would be forgiven (Matt., ch. 6). That statement is
made on the basis of the fact that, in Matthew, the Kingdom of
Heaven, the forgiving context, is present in Jesus Christ himself.

The final word about the nature of the context of forgiveness
follows as a corollary from the presence of the Kingdom. Bultmann calls attention to it when he says that the work of forgiveness — which is removal of the effect of sin and reconciliation
with God — is already accomplished.[16] It is not something for the
future. It is a completed fact. That is why it needs to be not
promised but proclaimed. The problem is not for people to be
forgiven but for people to discover the context of the forgiveness
that they already have.

The total view of forgiveness as a context is portrayed in the
beginning of The Gospel According to Mark in the story of the
man who was a paralytic. Recall that this man was on a stretcher
outside the house where Jesus was speaking in Capernaum. Jesus
was apparently on the second floor, and a great crowd blocked all

the entryways. Hence, the four men took the paralytic on the stretcher, carried him up an outside stairway, and let him down through the roof into the room where Jesus sat. The Scripture reads, " When Jesus saw *their* faith, he said to the paralytic, ' My son, your sins are forgiven.' " This, obviously, upset the scribes, who said that God alone could forgive. Thereupon, Jesus said to the sick man, " Rise, take up your pallet and go home." To everyone's amazement, he did.

First, there is here the common recognition of the contextual nature of forgiveness. This is precisely what bothered the scribes. Forgiveness could come only in the context of God; how, then, could it come in the context of Jesus? Second, there is the proclaimed nature of this context. Jesus began by telling the paralytic, " Your sins are forgiven." That is proclamation. Third, the very proclamation is evidence of the presence of the forgiveness. It was not something distant or in the future. It was something already accomplished. Fourth, it is a mediated context. Interestingly, Mark gives both the personal and corporate aspects of the mediation. Clearly, it is mediated personally through Jesus. However, note also that prior to Jesus' proclamation, Mark reports, " And when Jesus saw *their* faith." It was not the faith of the man, but the faith of the corporate group, that also mediated this forgiveness. Their intercession in bringing the man before Jesus was of primary importance.

There is one element in this story that has not been mentioned. It is the concluding statement about the paralytic. " He rose, and immediately took up the pallet and went out before them all." Where does this fit in the experience of forgiveness? *This* was the act of making forgiveness real for the man himself. It was the instrumentation by which the forgiveness became real to him. His act leads us, therefore, to the second pole in the dynamic understanding of forgiveness, viz., the instrumental nature of forgiveness.

The prime question that relates to this second pole asked, " *What is the instrument by which a person makes real the experience of forgiveness as a context?* " As one moves through the Scripture, the instrumentation of forgiveness seems to be related to three factors: the attitude of the individual, the act of God, and the symbolization of both in an expressive act.

The attitude of the individual, which is part of the instrumentation of making forgiveness real, might well be called a suffering attitude. Experience in pastoral care or in the use of the confessional indicates a universal element of struggle on the part of the person involved. This sense of suffering is sometimes made a focal point — as in certain monastic disciplines (e.g., the Qumran community shows a dimension of this in its discipline).[17] The sense of suffering is sometimes that which simply seems to accompany the process of forgiveness — such as the effort of the four men to carry the paralytic to Jesus. Nevertheless, it is always present. It costs something to make forgiveness real. Each person has to want it.

In the course of the Old Testament, confession, contrition, repentance, and conversion emerge as the elements that form the attitude of the individual to his need. Jeremiah expressed this poetically when he wrote: " We acknowledge our wickedness, O Lord, and the iniquity of our fathers, for we have sinned against thee." The psalmist wrote, " I wait for the Lord, my soul waits " (Ps. 130:5). There must be confession of guilt or of the need for God.

With this, the New Testament emphasizes the concept of positive confession. Positive confession is awareness not only of one's need but of one's new strength and new discovery. Peter *confesses,* " Thou art the Christ." Paul speaks of confessing with one's mouth the Lord Jesus (Rom., ch. 10). Jesus is disturbed when ten lepers are healed and only one returns to give thanks. His concern was not for gratitude or politeness. Awareness of the need for positive confession makes forgiveness real. Therefore, it is only to the one leper who gave thanks that Jesus says, " Your faith has made you well " (Luke 17:19).

A sense of contrition seems to have been central in the suffering attitude. Psalm 51 expressed this mood when it said, " For I know my transgressions, and my sin is ever before me." The context of forgiveness gives one the freedom and the courage to see the true nature of the sin that is before one. Seeing the nature of one's guilt is one of the means by which the forgiveness becomes real, for the individual is clear about that for which he needs to be forgiven. Along with sorrow for the guilt goes repentance and conversion. That is, with contrition there goes the desire not to commit the sins again. There is a move away from that which is sinful.

In the New Testament, the difference is not that any point is added to the aspects of the suffering attitude. It is that these are all focused in relation to Christ. The parable of the Pharisee and the publican (wherein the sinner asked God to be merciful, but the Pharisee thanked God that he was not as other men) indicates the need for the suffering attitude. Yet, in the New Testament, this suffering attitude on the part of people no longer is in terms of a proclaimed law that makes people weep (as in Nehemiah) nor an imposed ritual that people must follow in the church. Rather, the suffering attitude, in all its expressions, becomes centered in Christ. Before him, Peter says, " Depart from me, for I am a sinful man, O Lord."

The second factor in the instrumentation of forgiveness is the act of God. In the Old Testament, this act was seen as God in history. It might have been the parting of the Red Sea, the burning of the bush before Moses, the drying up of the Jordan so that the Israelites could pass over, the exile, or the return. In the New Testament, the act of God that is the instrument of making forgiveness real is the redemptive act of Christ. " For the Son of man also came not to be served but to serve, and to give his life as a ransom for many." (Mark 10:45.) [18]

In the New Testament, the cross of Christ, then, becomes the instrumentation for realizing forgiveness. Jesus is important not because of what he did with regard to the past but, as Bultmann observes, because of the promise for the future and the present.[19] Through Christ, forgiveness becomes a living experience.

Biblically, the third factor in the instrumentation of forgiveness is an expressive act on the part of the individual. Specifically, at the opening of Mark, this is the paralytic taking up his bed and walking.

The most clearly stated instrument for making forgiveness real is the act of forgiving others. The Dead Sea Scrolls contain an enlightening document on this point. That document, the Manual of Discipline, has a rule which reads, " You shall reprove your neighbor, lest you bear sin because of him." [20] Why? Because the Qumran community to which the manual refers had a deep awareness of the involvements we have in each other. If one man saw another commit a sin and did nothing about it, he was as guilty of that sin as the person who had committed it. What could he do? He could report it to the leader. However, the community seemed to have a strong sense of the priesthood of all believers. Therefore, one did the reporting *only* if personal conversation failed.

Under Christ, this same awareness of the responsibility and interinvolvement of one with another was carried a step farther. If forgiveness was that which released a man from the effect of sin, it was necessary to forgive the brother in order to give him that release. If the Qumran society correctly held that a man was involved in the sin of another merely by his awareness of it, then Jesus was right in requiring forgiveness of the brother in order to be released oneself. For if another man's sin is my sin, then another man's freedom is also my freedom. This is why the Lord's Prayer can, and must, read, " Forgive us our debts, as we forgive our debtors." It is instrumentally impossible to experience the reality of forgiveness apart from forgiving others.

Not only personally forgiving others, but also the proclamation of forgiveness, is an instrument of forgiveness. When the disciples were trying to heal an epileptic boy, their failure helped them to recognize their lack of awareness of forgiveness. The command of Jesus to go " make disciples of all nations " carries with it the promise, " Lo, I am with you always." The command can carry that promise, for one of the means by which the context of the forgiving Christ is made real is the proclaiming of that Christ. Hence, Ps. 51 describes the total experience of realizing forgiveness. It begins with the deep awareness of guilt and ends with the words, " Then I will teach transgressors thy ways," and " O Lord, open thou my lips, and my mouth shall show forth thy praise." When one discovers how to proclaim forgiveness by his lips and his mouth, forgiveness becomes real in a new way.

Along with forgiving others, the " sacrificial cultus " — i.e., the liturgy — stands out as another Biblical means of making forgiveness real. It is as important as the forgiving of others and proclaiming forgiveness.

It is true, as stated earlier, that whenever forgiveness as a context is reduced to forgiveness as a means, there is need for a reformation. Unfortunately, however, many have understood this reformation to mean throwing out the instrument altogether. It is clear from Scripture that although certain instruments may be inadequate and others may be bad, there always has to be an instrumentation by which forgiveness becomes real. There has to be a means by which the forgiveness can be expressed and brought to the awareness of the person involved.

In the Old Testament, there is reference to Moses holding up a serpent in the wilderness (Num. 21:9). That was an instrument and also a means of making people free from death. In the New Testament, Jesus said that even as the serpent was lifted up, so must the Son of Man be lifted up. His death on the cross, too, was to be an instrument of forgiveness. In the liturgy of the Temple, there was the sacrifice. These were instruments, and the death of Jesus is seen as analogous in that sense too. Today, after the death of Jesus, what is the instrument that represents this release? It is the Lord's Supper. The Letter to the Hebrews might be described as the book of the instrumentation of forgiveness. Chapter 9, verse 18, observes that, from the first, the covenant (the context of forgiveness) was not ratified without the shedding of blood. The Lord's Supper speaks of " the new covenant in my blood." And The Letter to the Hebrews then goes so far as to say, " Without the shedding of blood there is no forgiveness of sins " (Heb. 9:22). Hence, forgiveness may well mean to lighten and to remove the effect of sin. However, that does not just happen. The freedom to be newly creative, which is the realization of forgiveness, comes only when there is that instrumentation which makes it real. Liturgy, properly understood, is just such an expression.

Finally, there is a corporate aspect to the expressive act of the individual. " If you forgive the sins of any, they are forgiven," said Jesus. One of the instruments that makes forgiveness a reality is hearing a person say, " I forgive you." From the previous chapter, we know that this has to be one who is in a position to do the forgiving. The church, as the corporate body of Christ, is in that position. The Dead Sea Scrolls again throw light on this point. From them comes the hint that in the Lord's Supper, it is not the elements themselves that are important, but it is the sharing of them that makes real the presence of the Lord's body.[21] The priest, in offering the elements, is making forgiveness real. The church member, in passing the elements to the person next to him, is making the forgiveness real. So important is the corporate nature of the Sacrament that Paul understandably is disturbed at the way in which it was used in Corinth. He had to tell the Corinthians: " Wait for one another." (I Cor. 11:33.)

III   FORGIVENESS AS FREEDOM

We come, now, to the third and last question that pertains directly to forgiveness: " What is the nature of the forgiveness itself? " It was earlier postulated that forgiveness is that which gives freedom to be newly creative. Is this view of the nature of the field of forgiveness consistent with the view of forgiveness expressed in the Bible? When forgiveness in the Bible is looked at from the concern of pastoral theology and as a pastorally theological word, the answer is " Yes." This is not to say that the Biblical image and the twentieth-century image are the same. It is to say that the views are consistent and refer to the same basic experience.

In the Old Testament, much could be cited to show that freedom is at the heart of the nature of forgiveness. Here, only two examples will be given: The Book of Ezra and Ps. 51.

In The Book of Ezra, the Hebrew nation is found in the midst of the tension that came with rebuilding Jerusalem. The drama of the book centers on the question, " Will or will not the Hebrews have the freedom to build? " In the seventh month, the people gathered together and began to make offerings in accord with the liturgy. This was before the Temple was even started. When the adversaries of the builders then saw the foundation being laid, they tried to incite Darius against the Hebrews by telling falsehoods about Hebrew motives. The fifth chapter of the book tells how those who were obstructing the building came to

Jerusalem and started harassment. Ezra then reads: " But the eye of their God was upon the elders of the Jews, and they did not stop them till a report should reach Darius." (Ezra 5:5.) In that passage the context of God's presence is clearly identified with freedom — particularly the freedom to build. (The Book of Nehemiah demonstrates the same point for the same period.

In Ps. 51, the fourteenth verse begins, " Deliver me from blood-guiltiness, O God. . . ." The word for deliverance is the Hebrew *yesha*. It means deliverance or aid. It is a form of the Hebrew word *yasha* which means freedom.[22] Thus, salvation from sin is seen here not as healing or as wholeness, but as freedom.

The importance of freedom is also seen in the New Testament. There, as in the Old, the symbol of God's relationship with his people is the marriage. In the New Testament, when Jesus speaks of marriage, he says, " For this reason a man shall leave his father and mother and be joined to his wife, and the two shall become one." Why must the man leave his father and mother? Simply because he wants to create a new family. The marriage is a symbol of the new creation. Before he can do that, however, he must be genuinely free from the " old " family. Hence, in the entire Bible, freedom is basic to the experience that is described as forgiveness in the context of God.

The history of the development of the Hebrew understanding of God also supports the view that forgiveness makes creation possible. It is to be remembered that the early view of God in the Old Testament is a pastoral one. It is the view of Yahweh, before whom Adam sinned. It is the view of Yahweh the leader and redeemer. It is out of the atmosphere of understanding God as a redeemer that God is seen as a creator. In point of time, God indeed created man before he had to forgive him. From the standpoint of human experience, however, man needs redemption before he can be creative.[23] Creation in the Old Testament depends on the redemptive act of God.

In the New Testament, Paul speaks of the new creation. As with the Old Testament, this too depends on redemption. The statement in his letter to the Romans indicates that Paul, in talking about creation and being in Christ, is referring to the same dynamic that I identify as the essence of forgiveness. The passage reads as follows: " For the creation was subjected to futility, not of its own will but by the will of him who subjected it in hope; because the creation itself will be set free from its bondage to decay and obtain the glorious liberty of the children of God" (Rom. 8:20-22). Being set free from bondage to decay in order to be " the creation " is precisely what I have identified as the experience of " realized forgiveness."

Further, in his letter to the church at Corinth, Paul identifies the experience of being " in Christ " both with being a new creation and with being free from the effect of one's sins. Thus he writes: " If any one is in Christ, he is a new creation; the old has passed away, behold, the new has come. All this is from God, who through Christ reconciled us to himself and gave us the ministry of reconciliation; that is, God was in Christ reconciling the world to himself, not counting their trespasses against them, and entrusting to us the message of reconciliation." (II Cor. 5:17-19.)

Not to have trespasses counted against one is, again, freedom. Paul uses the word *ktisis* for " creation," which is also the word for " foundation." He uses the word *kainos* for " new," which, according to Trench, does not mean new in terms of time but new in terms of quality.[24] Hence, here as in his letter to the Romans, Paul is referring to that dynamic experience of freedom which I identify as the essence of forgiveness. Further, the identification of this newness as a qualitative newness shows the Biblical correlation with the new personality spoken of in the previous chapter. We may say, then, that whether Paul is talking to the Corinthians, or whether a twentieth-century pastor is talking to a parishioner, they are talking about the same thing, in terms of pastoral theology.

Two matters should be clarified before this discussion of the nature of forgiveness is concluded. Something should be said about the relation of understanding to forgiveness, and then about the relation of freedom to discipline.

It is often said that a person needs to understand in order to forgive. Mrs. A, whose case was mentioned in the opening chapter, related an instance that had happened some fifteen years earlier with her husband. " It suddenly came to me," she said, " that I now understand why he did it; and now I can forgive him."

Parallel to this experience is that of the two men on the road to Emmaus. As they were walking, they did not recognize Jesus. Jesus then interpreted to them everything in the Scripture. After that, they sat down, Jesus broke bread, and they suddenly realized that they were in the presence of the Savior. Does not this suggest that understanding is essential in making forgiveness possible? Should it not be given as a third pole in the field?

To both questions, the answer is " No." Why is it that Mrs. A took so many years to come to the point where she could forgive that particular act on the part of her husband? The " act " was nothing of great significance. What he did could have been understood long before it was. The difference was in a new factor: Mrs. A was now, herself, in the context of forgiveness. (She was in therapy.) The context of forgiveness made it possible for her to understand; her act of forgiving was the instrument by which she fulfilled the experience.

The same is true of the disciples. Before they understood what had happened, they were within the presence of Jesus. He was the context of forgiveness. That context led to the freedom to understand. The breaking of bread with Jesus was the instrument that made it real.[25] Thus, to answer the question as to whether or not forgiveness precedes understanding, it initially must be decided which part of forgiveness one has in mind. Basically, being forgiven comes first. If, however, one refers to the instrumentation, then understanding *may* sometimes come first.[26]

Parents usually ask how forgiveness and freedom are related to discipline. Discipline is sometimes thought of as an instrument of forgiveness and sometimes as a part of the context of forgiveness. By way of example, the Book of Discipline of The United Presbyterian Church U.S.A. speaks of administrative discipline and judicial discipline. The first pertains to the context of a church. The second pertains to reuniting an offender within the context.

The danger of rejecting a given instrument of discipline as inadequate and of emphasizing the context of discipline is moral chaos. At the time of Paul, again during the Reformation, and again in the present day, the forgiveness that is a basic part of freedom can be interpreted as the freedom to do as you like. If it is genuine freedom, it is clearly the freedom at least to make a mistake. It is, in part, for this reason that emphasis is put on the law and that Martin Marty speaks of forgiveness as the "hidden discipline." It is, in part, for this reason that Bonhoeffer speaks of the need for obedience. There is clear need for the warning of these men. The freedom of the gospel is not the freedom to do what you like.

Within the Scripture, there is also a clear sense of discipline in forgiveness. One must be careful, however, not to confuse the discipline with the instrumentation of forgiveness. That is what happens in Marty's presentation when he states that forgiveness is not possible apart from the law. In our society, he says, we need to start from law.[27] This reasoning suffers the error of being motivated by inadequacies or dangers in the present day — even though "these dangers" in our society are real. Forgiveness must not be understood on the basis of reaction to our problems but in terms of life as it is. The position that Marty takes forces him to say later that "the Law accuses, it does not save."[28] This is wrong. When understood as an instrument by which forgiveness becomes real, precisely the reverse is true. The law is one of the means by which saving forgiveness can come into one's awareness.

In much of the rest of his book, there is considerable agreement between what Marty says and what I have said. There is agreement, that is, until the point at which he defines the nature of the hidden discipline. He writes:

The alternative is not the external discipline of Old Law or new custom. The alternative is the Spirit-given vision of the Christlike life, exposed, unsheltered in the middle of the world.[29]

The value of his statement is that he recognizes the difference between a dynamic view of life and a legalistic view. He recognizes that Christianity can be as legalistic and irrelevant as any other religion. He recognizes that the guide for one's life is not relationship to law but relationship to a person — the person of Jesus Christ. The error in the statement, as I see it, is that the discipline of forgiveness is not the discipline of obedience to the will of Christ. Obedience to the will of Christ is indeed a discipline and a Christian virtue, but it is not the discipline *imposed* by forgiveness. Rather, it is the discipline that is *made possible* by forgiveness. Marty himself asserts this point when he says that we must "increase holiness on earth through these two means, the Christian church and the forgiveness of sins." [30] It is the identification of forgiveness with the instrumental nature of forgiveness that leads to error. For the discipline of forgiveness is not related to forgiveness as an instrument but as a context. No one is bound to any means of expressing forgiveness. No one is bound to old law, to new social custom, or even to a "vision of the Christlike life." For the problem is to be sure that the Christlike vision is, indeed, Spirit-given and not just the projection of our own desires.

Therefore, I believe that the discipline that is the hidden discipline of forgiveness must be understood in relation not to the instrumentation but to the context. In Mal. 1:6, God says: "A son honors his father, and a servant his master. If then I am a father, where is my honor?" In v. 10 God continues: "I have no pleasure in you, . . . and I will not accept an offering from your hand." The complaint in the prophecy is against an inadequate instrumentation of forgiveness and a lack of regard for the context of forgiveness. If one is to be free, whole, saved, restored — or whatever word is chosen — one must discipline oneself to stand in the context of God and find the instrumentation that makes the context real. The freedom that comes is not freedom from the context of God but freedom from bondage to false instrumentalities of that context. It is this which leads to the opportunity for a "Spirit-given vision" and the ensuing discipline.

IV FORGIVENESS EXPRESSED AS STRENGTH

In the preceding sections of this chapter, I have not discussed the word "strength." I believe it deserves special attention at this point. The desire for strength has been a dominant theme in some cultures and during some ages of history. The experience of strength is one of the meanings that the Bible has attached to what I am calling "realized forgiveness." To a degree, "strength" has been a concern in all times and all cultures. Today, for example, the wish for strength is reflected in the fact that our age is called "the age of anxiety." The slogan means that our time is characterized by loss of energy and strength through nervous disintegration. There is need for strong people. Again and again parishioners will say, " I'm tired." Advertisements repeatedly strike at the problem of being " run down, irritable." " We call it ' tired blood,' " says one commercial. Internationally, there is the call for strong nations. " Keep America strong " is the battle cry. United Nations Secretary-General U Thant, in a speech on June 27, 1963, predicted that the future would see four great world powers: Russia, a common market Europe, China, and the United States. He said that planning for the future should be in regard to the fact of these " strong " nations.

Strength, as a fruit of forgiveness, is a recurring motif in the Bible. Psalm 32 identifies it in its third verse: " When I declared not my sin, my body wasted away." This means that strength comes from wholeness, peace, at-one-ment with oneself, one's neighbor, and one's God. Paul spoke of a true strength " when I am weak." This also means that the strength man wants is not to be identified with just physical power but with a personal relationship.

There is also abundant evidence that lack of strength is related to sin and recovery of it to forgiveness. When Adam and Eve sinned, they found themselves in a weakened condition before God. They were cast out from the peace of the Garden of Eden. David, in the psalms that he wrote, and the authors of the other psalms suggested this at every turn. " My feet had almost stumbled . . . until I went into the sanctuary of God," says Ps. 73. Or contrast the personalities of David and Saul. Saul was a man of power whose strength was lost by jealousy, by making important what is not important, and by losing the forgiveness of God. David became stronger and stronger as the awareness of God's forgiveness deepened in him. When the child of his unholy relation with Bathsheba was dying, he mourned. After the child died, David ceased his mourning. When asked why, David's reply showed considerable insight. He emerged as a stronger person than he was when, as a military commander, he pulled the strings that made Bathsheba his wife. David's life ended as a life of strength, whereas Saul's life ended as a life of disintegration.

The motif of strength is carried forward by the prophets. Isaiah spoke of renewing strength and mounting up like the eagles. Jesus expressed it too. " Thy sins are forgiven " was followed by " take up thy bed and walk " — an act of strength. And for Paul and the early church, the peace and oneness of the Corinthian church was directly related to being a new creature in Christ.

What, however, is the relationship between " freedom " and " strength "? Are these contradictory ways of looking at forgiveness? The answer is " No." Both " freedom " and " strength " are parts of the picture of forgiveness. This is true both in the Bible and in the modern day. The distinction is that freedom usually refers to what helps to make forgiveness possible, whereas strength refers to what makes it actual. " Freedom " is a word that is identified with the context of forgiveness more than the instrument. " Strength " is a word that is identified more with the instrument of awareness of forgiveness than with the context.

However, there is a danger in this word " strength." The danger is that the total experience of forgiveness will come to be identified with health, success, and power. In the Bible, the symbol of strength was often identified with something physical — such as the golden calf. Nevertheless, this identification of strength with health, or strength with the total experience of forgiveness, is one of the understandings of forgiveness that is rejected by the Bible. Moses had the golden calf destroyed. When it was said of Jesus, " He saved others; he cannot save himself," Jesus indeed did not recover from the cross. Strength is not understood, Biblically, in this physical sense.

V   THE DEVELOPMENT OF THE IDEA OF FORGIVENESS

The concept of forgiveness has developed throughout the history of Biblical thought along certain lines. These lines are like developmental threads that can be traced through the Bible. These developmental threads can be reduced to four.

Initially, there is the thread of movement from a generally legalistic view of forgiveness to a generally dynamic view. This is seen in the development of the idea of God as just Yahweh, a tribal lord, to the Elohim who creates the heavens and the earth. This is to say that God as the context of forgiveness starts out being seen anthropomorphically and ends by being seen dynamically.

The move from a legalistic to a dynamic view of forgiveness is also seen in the shift concerning judgment. Judgment is seen as an act. It later comes to be seen as a matter of relationship. The Hebrew word for judgment (*mishpāṭ*) means the administration of judgment.[31] It is often used in connection with the word *tsadaq,* which means righteousness or right-relatedness. Early in the Bible, judgment is understood as administrative acts carried out by a king. Thus, Jezebel told Ahab, in effect, that he was right because he was king. Hence, judgment has something of a negative, arbitrary, and destructive quality. By the time of Second Isaiah and Jeremiah, however, a positive dimension is added to judgment. " Keep justice, and do righteousness," we read (Isa. 56:1), "for my house shall be called a house of prayer for all peoples " (v. 7). This represents a shift in which judgment and righteousness have to do positively with a relationship of oneness with God and man. And Deuteronomy, as mentioned earlier, takes great pains to suggest the relational aspect of judgment and law when it says, " The Lord spoke with you face to face " (Deut. 5:4). Judgment, and forgiveness as it relates to judgment, thus comes to be seen dynamically and relationally.

This same development is found in the New Testament in the transition from the view of the Pharisees to the view of Christ. The law is made for man, not man for the law, Christ said.

Many other instances of this particular development can be found. The level at which it will be found depends on both the period and the culture. Yet, it will be found.

The second thread of development is the shift from a cultic view of forgiveness to a relational view. In the early days of the Hebrew nation, the cultic laws were paramount. They are found in great detail in Leviticus. That position moved to the call in Joel 2:13 and elsewhere, " Rend your hearts and not your garments." In the New Testament, the same shift is seen in the conflict between Paul and the Judaizers. The latter saw deeds that must be done, whereas Paul emphasized relationship to God over the cultic practices of circumcision and diet.

The problem here is that the cult, as an instrumentation of forgiveness, is necessary. Yet, the cult as an instrumentation can quickly and easily be identified with forgiveness as a context. It must constantly be reasserted that, since a context needs an instrument to make the forgiveness real, there is always the danger that every expression of the context will be reduced to nothing more than an instrument. This is the battle not only throughout Scripture but throughout the history of faith.

The third thread is the way in which the understanding of death develops. There is a heightening of the thought that death leads to life. Forgiveness gives the freedom to be a new, live creature. The motion is always from death to life. In the Old Testament, this was seen on a terribly primitive level. Joshua, ch. 7, tells of some Israelites who, after a victory, took for themselves some " devoted things." To atone for doing this, each person of Israel was to come forward, and those who were found with devoted things were to be put to death. " He who is taken with the devoted things shall be burned with fire, he and all that he has, because he has transgressed the covenant of the Lord, and because he has done a shameful thing in Israel." (Josh. 7:15.) Freedom, the experience of forgiveness, came with the actual death of the person involved. This same primitive approach can be found elsewhere in the days even up to Saul.

A higher view is found in the life of David. David sinned in putting Uriah, Bathsheba's husband, in the front line in order that he would be killed. When the stratagem worked, and David married Bathsheba, they had a son. The son became sick. David repented, went into sackcloth and ashes, and did everything he could to atone for his deed. The child died. The child's death was interpreted as atonement for David's act, but it is an advance over the incident from Joshua in that the child was not made an altar sacrifice.

The highest level of the view of death leading to life is found in the death of Christ. What has happened to Christ is interpreted as being what each person must do spiritually if he is to live. Mary is told that a sword will pierce her own soul also (Luke 2:35). Paul says that when we are baptized, we are baptized into his death. Forgiveness as an experience of freedom does not come by physical death but by that spiritual death in which we bury what is past and move on to the future.

The fourth and final thread that runs through Scripture is the shift from " Repent and be forgiven " to " The kingdom of God is at hand." In the early Old Testament ritual, repentance was pretty much for purification. Between the prophets and the priests, there was a constant battle. The former were striving for, and often getting, a deeper view of forgiveness in relation to repentance. The latter were holding to the cult. The New Testament, with John the Baptist, presents the positive note of seeing the context of forgiveness as present, realized, and the means of entry into a new life. Thus, the gospel begins with John announcing that context: " The kingdom of God is at hand."

How one understands the relation between " Repent and be forgiven " and " the kingdom of God is at hand " depends on whether or not forgiveness is an act to be repeated constantly or an attitude that is once and for all. This problem becomes increasingly significant in our day in the discussion between Thomistic theology and Calvinism over the significance of one's confession of faith in Christ. Once confession has been made, can one fall out of the state of grace?

In the proposal that has been presented here, the answer depends on whether or not reference is made to forgiveness as a context or an instrument. Insofar as forgiveness is a context, one realizes the forgiveness and is in an attitude of being forgiven " once and for all." Insofar as forgiveness is an instrument, it is an act repeated again and again in order to make the " once and for all " context real in each succeeding area of human experience.

VI CONCLUSION

From this review of forgiveness in the Scripture, we can conclude that the dynamic approach as a method does make sense. It is adequate for understanding the meaning of Scripture in relation to pastoral theology. It also seems clear that, in Scripture, whenever forgiveness as a real element in the lives of people was lost, a reformation was necessary. At this point, I would go a step farther and say also that every reformation is an attempt to discard an inadequate instrumentation of forgiveness and to gain an adequate one. From this, it seems that the problem in forgiveness is not so much whether or not people find it realized in worship, confession, small groups, mass meetings, or private worship. Rather, the important matter is to find the basic instrumentality that makes the context of forgiveness real for oneself, and to use it. This point, from the Bible, coincides with the test results of the previous chapter.

Further, the preceding discussion has answered the question, " Why is Christ needed? " and it has clarified the relationship of the New Testament to the Old. Christ is needed precisely because in no other way is there sufficient mediation of the context of forgiveness. He is needed because the cross as an instrument of God allows man to see that context. In the Old Testament, there is the battle between those who would see forgiveness as an instrument alone and those who would recognize the aspect of forgiveness as a context. In the New Testament, this battle is resolved. Christ, within himself, brings together both the contextual and instrumental dimensions of forgiveness. He is the instrument that makes real the Kingdom of God at hand. In his presence, one is either destroyed in this world (Judas went out and hanged himself) or freed from bondage to this world (Thomas said, " My Lord and my God "). Thus, as forgiveness is that which gives freedom to be a new creature, as forgiveness is that which gives the freedom to understand, and as forgiveness is at the heart of the gospel, so the New Testament is that which makes it possible to understand the Old. Without the realization of forgiveness, the Bible is unintelligible and irrelevant.

4

The Early Church in Search of Forgiveness

I INTRODUCTION

IN many ways, history could be written as the history of man's search to find forgiveness. This is particularly true of church history, and it is supremely true of the early church. However, in writing such a history, the historian would quickly run into a problem of semantics. Part of the difficulty in writing the previous chapters was the fact that people mean different things by forgiveness. Conversely, people easily describe the experience of forgiveness without ever referring to the word itself.

To see the significance of " forgiveness " in the development of the early church, the reader must recognize that the term " forgiveness " can be used in three ways. It can be used to describe a total experience. It can be used to describe a context. It can be used to describe a means by which something is accomplished (I have used the word " instrumentation ").

What has this look at " forgiveness " in the parish and in the Bible told us? It has said that, as a total experience, forgiveness refers to that dynamic experience which makes one free to be creative. There are two poles in this field. It is this whole experience to which I am referring when I use the phrase " realized forgiveness." It is an experience that has come alive. The previous chapters have said that forgiveness must be seen in this total sense.

When " forgiveness " is applied just to the context, it is referring to just one pole in the greater field of experience. This is the dimension of experience that precedes everything else. It is a given. None of us can do anything about it. We can reject it. We can accept it. We cannot ignore it. In this sense, forgiveness is God's gracious act and is mediated to us. I do not call this "realized," for it is not. Athanasius uses the analogy of the man who does not see the sun because he does not open his eyes. This is that kind of forgiveness. Like the sun, it encompasses everything, but one does not realize it unless one opens one's eyes. Hence, to this experience I give the direct name "forgiveness." It is what most people mean when they speak of "the forgiveness of God."

Usually, however, the popular use of the word "forgiveness" refers only to its third aspect. It is used of the means or the instrument by which we are made free from feelings of guilt. This is what brings the context into awareness. In describing personality, Carl Rogers says that the healthiest personality is the one that has been able to bring the most experiences into its awareness and adequately deal with them. The psychological instrument or means by which this is done is therapy. Acceptance is most often identified as the key part of therapy.

When most comparisons are made between psychotherapy and religion in terms of healing, the discussion takes place at this level. In this dimension, when forgiveness is understood in static and legal terms, religion does not come out very well. People feel that the church has nothing to offer, and psychiatry, psychoanalysis, or psychology are considered the places to turn for "real" help.

In opposition to psychiatric treatment, forgiveness as an instrument is sometimes presented in dynamic terms. Despite that, when forgiveness is seen just instrumentally, there is one of two results: religion and psychotherapy end in a standoff from each other or one is absorbed by the other. Consider these examples which are just two of several that show how the relation between religion and psychotherapy is either a standoff or a merger. The Order of Saint Luke is a movement within the institutional church that centers on faith healing. Even though some psychiatrists are involved, the central approach of this group is one of confession and forgiveness. The group has little to do with the other associations of ministers and doctors who are involved in healing (such as hospital chaplains in the Council for Clinical

Training movement). In the mind of the parishioner, the relation between psychologist and minister is a standoff. Whichever one works is fine.

The merger of psychology and religion is often seen in the membership of the Council for Clinical Training and the American Association for Religion and Psychiatry. In such groups, ministers improve their understanding of counseling. Usually, if they stay long enough with either of these groups, they move beyond the criticism I am now making. However, the orientation of their programs is so clinical that many identify forgiveness and acceptance as the same thing. A person learns counseling in order to be a better pastor. In my own experience, however, I discovered that I had identified too closely the work of counseling with the work of being a pastor. It was not until I began to ask serious questions about the nature of forgiveness that I came fully to sense the difference. This is a distinction that men such as Seward Hiltner and Granger Westberg have recognized; but generally we ministers have so centered our attention on the problem of freeing people from their guilts that we have seen forgiveness as an instrument and nothing else. The result is that in all theological camps and pastoral approaches, the nature of the church and of the ministry is unclear.

Hence, although forgiveness is usually thought of as an instrument, even when meant dynamically, I prefer not to use it in this regard at all. Unfortunately, I have not yet found a word that is adequate. " Symbol work " has meaning for me, but painful discussion has shown that it does not have much meaning for anyone else. The danger of the term " symbol work " is that it really belongs to that area of pastoral theology which Hiltner identifies as " communication."

As one perceives the nature of this confusion in today's church, the struggle in the early church suddenly becomes current. In different words, the fathers of the first centuries were involved in the same basic concerns that we share today. In fact, no other time in church history is more like ours than those early years. The world was relatively one world with two large divisions — East and West. The world was materialistic. It had great commerce. The prime difference between the churches of that day and those of our time is the form in which the concerns are expressed.

Hence, for my purposes here, each time I speak of forgiveness, I will identify which of its three aspects is meant.

II   THE EARLY CHURCH DEFINED

By the " early church," I mean the church from the time of Christ until it had lived long enough in history to show a definite pattern. To some, the " early church " means the primitive church. To others, it means the church up to the time of Gregory the Great — the period Kenneth Scott Latourette referred to as " The First Five Centuries." Although the life of one of the persons who concerns us does extend into the fifth century, my concern is not chronological either.

The span of this specific pattern is described by John T. McNeill in his definitive book *Medieval Handbooks of Penance.* In the introduction, he notes that, from the first, Christianity applied an austere set of standards for behavior. The worst offenses meant expulsion. In the early church, the chief feature of church discipline was its public character.[1] In the third and fourth centuries, penance became a growingly prominent feature of this public discipline. Various classes of penance came into being. There were the " weepers," who had to stay outside the door; the " hearers," who could enter the vestibule but had to remain standing ; the " kneelers," who could get into the sanctuary but had to remain on their knees; and, finally, the " costanders," who could join the regular congregation in the sanctuary but were not permitted to take Communion.[2]

In the West, particularly after Augustine, civil law had considerable influence on the penitential system. The rules included all civil crimes.[3] In the East, under Basil of Caesarea and with the development of the monastery, penitential laws also became codified. According to McNeill, this public penance was thought of, " not merely as a discipline for the restoration of the privileges of membership in the church, but as a means of supernatural grace overruling the consequences of sin and recovering the favor of God." [4]

In the typology that I have suggested, penance was the instrumentation of forgiveness. It was the means by which a person's forgiveness by God and oneness with God were made real. Then, as today, the popular mood centered on concern for an effective instrument that would relieve people from the consequences of their problems.

Through all of this time, however, penance was public. It was not until the sixth century that the practices of private confession and penance took form as we now have them.[5] Thus, the "definite pattern" by which I define the "early church" in this chapter carries us roughly to this new period. We center on the days of public confession and penance.

By the "early church," also, I do not mean the councils. This study within the field of pastoral theology is centered on the parish and the experience of men from the parish. In order to compare equals, the decisions of the councils should be compared with the decisions of our World Council of Churches assemblies or with the Second Vatican Council. The councils in any age may reflect the parish, but they are the church operating in an administrative capacity. Just as "symbol work" above really referred to that dimension of pastoral theology which is communication, so the councils refer to that dimension which is administrative. They are clearly related, but for the purpose of fair comparison and because they reveal little except by way of implication, they are omitted here.

It is often said that whenever one begins to read the early church fathers, one appears to be in an entirely different world from the world of the Bible. This is so, but not as much so as it first appears. The creeds also seem to represent an entirely different world from that of the church fathers. The creeds and the Scripture share the fact that they are the distillation of all the controversy and human concerns of the day. The Bible, as we have it, is the considered judgment, from many writings, as to what expresses *the* Word of God. The creeds, as we have them, are the judgment, from many expressions, as to what best represents the faith revealed in that Word of God. Thus, the jump from the Bible to the church fathers is not a jump from one world to another, but from one dimension of the world to another dimension of the same world. The world of the Bible, pictured in the preceding chapter, is the world of a proclaimed faith. The world of the church fathers, discussed in this chapter, is the world of a faith being experienced.

III THE SITUATION OF THE EARLY CHURCH

The situation of the early church can be described by one word: concern. This concern was reflected politically, intellectually, and religiously.

Politically, the church was concerned about persecution. Periods of persecution always lead to thoughts of the Second Coming. Apocalyptic literature grows. There is an emphasis on the future life rather than on the present. Periods of persecution also bring concern for the purity of the fellowship. There is the danger of informers coming from the outside. There is the danger of people within the fellowship compromising their principles. The organizational structure and practice of the church thus becomes important.

Intellectually, the early church was concerned about the relation between Hebrew thought and Greek thought. From the beginning, there was the process of the church becoming Hellenized. Adolf von Harnack says that this process did not end until the close of the third century.[6] Surely its effect was still seen in the fourth century.

A large part of coming to terms with Greek thought centered in the battles with Gnosticism. Gnosticism spoke of " the secrets of the holy path which are called ' gnosis.' " [7] *Gnōsis,* that Greek word which is related both to " knowledge " and to " becoming," was what enabled a person to know he had salvation. Gnosticism emphasized heaven. In the typology of forgiveness that has been set up, Gnosticism centered on the context of forgiveness. It did not bring heaven and earth together. It did not allow for the instrument that would make that forgiveness real. Hence, the challenge of the early church was to come to terms with the reality of that which is more than three dimensions, but not to deny what is in three dimensions. Gnostic thinking attempted to meet that challenge, but it failed because it bought heaven at the expense of earth. It did not redeem earth.

Religiously, the concern of the early church was to come to terms with law. This concern was expressed in relation to freedom. There was the desire for freedom from bondage to guilt and for freedom from bondage to law. This was a concern of both East and West in relation to Hebrew tradition. In a sense, the East met it by learning to interpret the Scripture by allegory. The West tried to meet it forensically or in the manner of the legal system of Rome.

The common denominator of all these concerns was the desire to find that which would leave the church — East or West — free to deal with political crises, the quest for knowledge, and religious expression. Sometimes it was overtly called a search for forgiveness. Sometimes it was not. Always, however, the dynamic experience in question was fundamentally the same.

IV THE BASIC SEARCH

That forgiveness was the basic quest can be documented if forgiveness is defined as that dynamic wherein one becomes free to be a new creature. In the early church, the search was for freedom to come to terms with life as life was found politically, intellectually, religiously, and emotionally.

A reading of the church fathers indicates that their search was for that which would allow integrity or wholeness in relation to the world view, as that view was understood. For example, the author of the Letter of Barnabas wanted people to have the ability to grow in their situation. " Since then He has renewed us by the forgiveness of sin," the author wrote, " He made us another product, and we have the soul of children as though He were creating us again." [8] This letter had considerable influence on both Clement of Alexandria and Origen. Here, at exactly the same time as many New Testament Scriptures were being written (ca. 70–100), Barnabas gives a description of the fruit of " realized forgiveness." The fruit is to be as one newly created within the situation where he was. This result is fundamental to the concern of the church.

The letter went on to speak of the covenant that God promised but that the people were not worthy to receive because of their sins. Therefore, " the Lord Himself gave it to us, as the people of inheritance, by suffering on our account." Once again, we are brought directly back to the typology of forgiveness that has emerged in the studies of the pastorate and of the Scripture. Barnabas is here speaking of forgiveness as a context (expressed in the covenant) that is mediated by Christ. As a suffering servant, Jesus also becomes the instrument for making that context real.

The history of what happened to the understanding of "realized forgiveness" is easily grasped in the light of the typology that has been mentioned. In the early church, there was awareness of the total experience of "realized forgiveness" with its two poles of context and instrumentation. Somewhere in the second century, appreciation of the full experience began to fade. Instead, the church tended to identify forgiveness with one or the other of the two poles.

Along with the author of the important Letter of Barnabas, Polycarp and Clement of Rome reflect the appreciation of the early church for the total experience of "realized forgiveness."

Polycarp was martyred ca. A.D. 155. His name is held in high esteem, for, according to tradition, he knew the apostle John. Polycarp was told to recant or be burned. Replied the martyr: "Eighty-six years have I served Him, and He has done me no wrong. How can I blaspheme my King who saved me?" Here is an expression of "realized forgiveness." The statement shows a total field of experience that has within it the two poles. The pole of context is expressed by reference to Christ as the one to be served. The pole of instrumentation is expressed by Polycarp speaking of Christ as the one who saves.

The Didache also demonstrates awareness of "realized forgiveness." It commanded: "You shall confess your offences in church, and shall not come forward to your prayers with a bad conscience. This is the way of life." [9] The church was the context, and the confession and coming forward were the instrument. Likewise, the so-called Second Epistle of Clement spoke of repentance being required in order to have goodness,[10] and Barnabas talked of the freedom to be creative that came from forgiveness: "When we received forgiveness of sins and put our hope in the Name [of Jesus], we were renewed, totally recreated; and so God truly dwells in us as in His habitation." [11]

The final document of the very early time of the church which should be mentioned is the Shepherd of Hermas. The Shepherd is an allegorical document that deals with two concerns — the problem of second repentance and the matter of Baptism. The date of the Shepherd is somewhat in question. It would be interesting to know the exact date, for that would be of help in identifying when the split in understanding the full nature of forgiveness began. Regardless, the Shepherd seems to be a transition between that time when forgiveness was understood in its fullest dimension and the time when either one polarity or the other became the center of concern.

The problem was that if a person were once forgiven and then sinned, could he be forgiven again? In view of our typology, this question suggests that the Shepherd identified forgiveness with the contextual pole — i.e., forgiveness as a context. Once this context has become real to a person's awareness, it is a contradiction in terms to speak of being unforgiven. From the contextual side, we are always within forgiveness. The concern of the Shepherd was to indicate in what way a person could then still sin and be forgiven again. In modern terms, the answer is that the awareness of forgiveness may indeed lapse as one moves out of the situation in which it was first made clear. Insofar as the instrumentality of forgiveness is concerned, the means by which forgiveness becomes real can and does appear repeatedly. It is the message of the Shepherd that second repentance is possible.[12] The possibility arises, however, only when the two poles of forgiveness are seen; and the repetition is in regard to the pole of instrumentation.

In another way, the Shepherd provides a link in the transition from the total to the partial view of forgiveness in the life of the church. It does it when discussing the relation of understanding to penance and forgiveness. In the controversy with the Gnostics, the matter of "understanding" was important. The Shepherd recognized the relationship and insisted that understanding was dynamically related.

I am in charge of penance, and give understanding to all who repent. Do you not think . . . that this very act of repentance is understanding: Repentance . . . is deep understanding. For the man who has sinned, then, understands that he has done evil before the Lord, the deed he commits enters into his heart and he repents.[13]

This statement reflects a sense of the dynamic view of the nature of forgiveness. The sharpness with which it speaks suggests that that view was becoming less clear in the life and thought of the church as a whole. There apparently was growing emphasis on understanding as a prerequisite of forgiveness, much as illustrated in the case of Mrs. A. The fact that the Shepherd had to speak to this point indicates concern over identifying forgiveness with one pole as opposed to the other.

Whether or not, then, its concept was correct, the underlying concern of the church in its earliest moments was forgiveness.

V   THE SPLIT

After the earliest days, a split began. In line with the typology, it may be identified as a split between East and West. In the East, the concern centered on forgiveness understood as a context. In the West, the concern centered on forgiveness understood as an instrument. As in all typologies, this point cannot be pushed too far. In both East and West there are some exceptions. In both East and West, every expression of forgiveness showed some awareness of the other dimension. The typology refers to a trend. Even in the most notable exceptions, the trend can be seen either in the direction of context or of instrumentation.

Under the Pax Romana, the West was concerned about law and structure. Due to the influence of the military, there was great emphasis on obedience. The obedience was not to God only, but to the authorities whom God had ordained. Throughout history, it is out of the West that there has come great concern for order and system. The Eastern church does not have great systems of theology in the sense that the Western church has them. The obedience of the West is not to God only, but to these systems and structures.

Since the law, the systems, and the structures are the means by which God is made real and effective in daily life, they are the instruments. It is thus no surprise that forgiveness in the West should come to center on the instrumentation pole. Wherever there is law, there is also guilt. Guilt is met by confession and then payment. In the East, there are disciplines and portrayals of the faith — symbols they are called. In the West, there are confessions. The greatest of these was the classic *The Confessions of Saint Augustine*.

Augustine has been chosen as the example from the West for several reasons. He represents the keenest understanding of forgiveness seen in the West during the rise of the early church. He was aware of both the context and the instrumentation of forgiveness. Yet his leaning was in the direction of instrumentation. He has been chosen also because he was far enough removed from the first two centuries to have some perspective on them. His life was surrounded by the background of scholarship, the influence of the monastics, and a structure of society that was sharply outlined. Because of the threat to Roman life in his day, Augustine was in a strategic historical position. Because of his background, he had the intellectual and personal tools with which to meet and speak from that position to that time. Perhaps supremely, Augustine has been chosen because, as Williston Walker wrote: " He was to be the father of much that was most characteristic in mediaeval Roman Catholicism. He was to be the spiritual ancestor, no less, of much in the Reformation." [14]

By a statement in the *Confessions,* Augustine shows that he is concerned with that central experience which this study defines as " realized forgiveness." He speaks of a time in which " I, still bound to the earth, refused to be Thy soldier; and was as much afraid of being freed from all embarrassments, as we ought to fear to be embarrassed. Thus with the baggage of the world was I sweetly burdened." [15] The dynamic of freedom from a burden is the central part of the experience that was important to Augustine as the experience of forgiveness. The dynamic of freedom was also threatening and fearful. These two elements have already been identified in the studies from pastoral care and the Scripture. In describing forgiveness, Augustine also showed some awareness of the two poles.

The difficulty with Augustine's picture of forgiveness was not unawareness of the contextual pole and its relation to freedom. Rather, it was his lack of attention to the contextual dimension.

Instead he centered on the way to make the freedom real — viz., the instrument. The instrumentation of forgiveness in Augustine was not a static and legalistic concept. The manner in which he wrote his *Confessions* reflects a vital sense of the instrumentation of forgiveness. All of that is good. However, Augustine tended to identify the contextual pole of experience with the theological statement of the grace of God. Hence, he removed the contextual from the dynamic of forgiveness itself. This meant that forgiveness would be identified primarily with the pole of instrumentation. From the standpoint of pastoral theology, this was a failure at the start — in the vestibule of theology — that could lead only to difficulties when Augustine came to certain of his theological arguments.

To see the basis for this observation about Augustine's understanding of forgiveness, consider three areas of his life: his personal struggle, his battle with the Pelagians, and his concern with the fall of the structure of Rome.

Hints as to his understanding of forgiveness can be found throughout the *Confessions*. His personal inward pilgrimage, however, is no more beautifully described than in the eighth book of the *Confessions*. There, he seems to pull together the facets of his experience; we see demonstrated the whole of "realized forgiveness" and we see the beginning emphasis on the instrument.

Augustine was born in 354 and died in 430. He lived something of a riotous life as a young man. He had a child by a concubine whom he never married. His mother seems to have had a rather strong influence in his life. Although he idealized her in his *Confessions,* there are hints that she may well have had an unwholesome and domineering effect upon him from which he needed to free himself. He seems to have moved in and out of a firm awareness of the Christian faith. For a time, he moved away from skepticism into Manichaeism. From that he moved back into skepticism. Ultimately, he came to the experience of forgiveness that is summarized in the eighth book of his *Confessions.*

In his conversion experience, he became conscious of the place of the instrumental nature of forgiveness. Augustine wrote that he went to talk to a faithful and understanding Christian named Simplicianus. In the course of the conversation, Augustine mentioned his interest in rhetoric and his admiration for a rhetorician in Rome, Victorinus. Simplicianus knew Victorinus and told Augustine that the great speaker had secretly been a Christian, but would not attend church. When Simplicianus had said he would not believe that Victorinus was a Christian until he went to the church of Christ, the rhetorician had replied, " Is it then the walls that make Christians? " [16]

This argument is not unknown today. Particularly in the Protestant tradition, we emphasize that being Christian is not to be identified with the institutional church. Victorinus would appear to be right; but the case study that Augustine gives proves the matter to be otherwise. Wrote Augustine:

After that, from reading and inquiry, he had derived strength, and feared lest he should be denied by Christ before the holy angels if he now was afraid to confess Him before men, and appeared to himself guilty of a great fault in being ashamed of the sacraments of the humility of Thy word, and not being ashamed of the sacrilegious rites of those proud demons, whose pride he had imitated and their rites adopted, he became bold-faced against vanity and shame-faced toward the truth, and suddenly and unexpectedly said to Simplicianus, . . . " Let us go to the church; I wish to be made a Christian." [17]

Within this experience, " the walls " become important for Augustine. The instrumentation of forgiveness was considered crucial. It may be observed that Augustine indeed reflected awareness of the contextual pole when he expressed impatience that " I entered not into Thy will and covenant, O my God." [18] Yet his passionate concern was, " How? " What was the instrumentation that would make the context real?

The answer comes at the end of Book 8. He heard the voice of a child say, " Take up and read." He remembered that the first monk, Antony, had done this and found the " how " of forgiveness in the admonition to " sell what thou hast and give to the poor." Thus, Augustine read and came upon the passage that said, " Not in rioting and drunkenness, not in chambering and wantonness, not in strife and envying; but put ye on the Lord Jesus Christ, and make not provision for the flesh, to fulfill the lusts thereof." [19] Instantly, he reported, all doubt vanished.

He then went and told two people. One was Alypius, a friend

who had gone with him to the garden. The other was his mother. The instrumentation that made the context real was the written word and the positive confession of his faith to others.

Note that the reality of the experience involved all the points that have previously been mentioned under the rubric of " realized forgiveness." The fundamental nature of the experience was freedom from doubt and freedom from bondage to the passions of the flesh.[20] It was freedom to have the " power of a new life," as he states in the next book of his *Confessions*. With this polarity, there was the contextual nature of forgiveness. For what did the Scripture do but call him to that context, by a proclaiming of that context, when it said, " Put ye on the Lord Jesus Christ "? The context of forgiveness enabled Augustine to look toward himself.[21] All this was accompanied by considerable suffering. He speaks of " silent trembling " and " of this great strife of my inner dwelling." [22] Add to that, then, the instrumentation of the context, and Augustine has given a picture of the totality of "realized forgiveness." Unfortunately, Augustine did not see both aspects of the picture he drew. So concerned was he to reach forgiveness, and so much in the tradition of the West, that he came to identify this experience not with the context *and* the instrumentation, but only with the latter.

It was in the Pelagian controversy that this identification became clear. It would be going too far afield to discuss the elements of that controversy here. However, as stated in the previous chapter, unless one comes at the questions of systematic theology through the vestibule of pastoral theology, one becomes hopelessly bogged down. Free will and providence will come to be opposite horns of a dilemma instead of two aspects of a greater experience. This is precisely what happened with Augustine.

In his *Admonition and Grace,* which was written for some monastics who were disturbed by Augustine's anti-Pelagian views, " grace " is clearly expressed. Augustine says:

If grace is lacking, the law is there simply to make culprits and to slay; for this reason, the Apostle said: " The letter killeth, the spirit giveth life." He, therefore, who uses the law according to the law learns from it good and evil, and, trusting not in his own strength, has recourse to grace, which enables him to avoid evil and to do good. But when has a man recourse to grace, except when the steps of a man are directed by the Lord and he delighteth in His way? Therefore, even the desire for the help of grace is itself the beginning of grace; about it he said: " And I said: Now have I begun; this is a change due to the right hand of the Most High." [23]

It is the context of the Lord that both changes the effect of law and is necessary for life. It is grace that makes even the desire possible. All this is precisely the language that describes the context of forgiveness.

In this passage Augustine has identified grace with the context of forgiveness. But grace and forgiveness are not the same. Forgiveness as a context may be a result of the grace of God, but each is something in and of itself. That grace is much more than forgiveness is shown by Augustine himself. In the Enchiridion he goes on to say that " even eternal life itself, which is surely the reward of good works, is called by the Apostle, grace of God: ' For the wages of sin is death,' he says, ' but the grace of God is life everlasting, Christ Jesus our Lord.' " [24] With this statement there is no disagreement. It is a demonstration that forgiveness as a context and the grace of God are related but not the same. Forgiveness comes from God's grace and leads to the grace of life everlasting. However, forgiveness is not itself life everlasting. Each speaks to the other but should not be identified. Thus Augustine moved to identify forgiveness primarily with the pole of instrumentation. That always leads to failure in grasping the total dynamic of " realized forgiveness."

This failure led directly to his being both right and wrong in his debate with Pelagius. Augustine insisted that with regard to grace, man is not free. In this sense he was correct. Man has nothing whatever to do with the context of forgiveness. With regard to making that forgiveness real, however, Pelagius had a point. Man is free to choose the instrument. He is free to decide which way he will go after he has chosen it, and he is free to decide not to choose it at all.

At this point in his thought, rejection of the contextual side is not complete. In fact, it never is. Awareness of the context of forgiveness is shown in the Enchiridion; but it is the emphasis on instrumentation that is paramount. In speaking of the importance of penance, Augustine said that the forgetting of penance was often a weakness.[25] Therefore,

> . . . whoever believes that sins are not forgiven in the Church, and despises this great gift of divine grace, and ends his last day in this obstinancy of mind, is guilty of that unforgivable sin against the Holy Spirit, in whom Christ forgives sin.[26]

If the church is that which mediates the context, he is right. Unfortunately with this statement Augustine reduces the church to the institutional instrument wherein forgiveness becomes real.

Augustine's emphasis on instrumentation can also be seen politically in his reaction to the fall of Rome. In *The City of God* he wrote: " The whole use, then, of things temporal has a reference to this result of earthly peace in the earthly community, which in the city of God it is connected with earthly peace." [27] The purpose of the institution is to be the instrumentation of peace. The evidence that the church is this instrumentation is seen in the power of the keys. This power, Christ granted to the church:

> So that whatever it might loose upon earth would be loosed in heaven, and whatever it might bind on earth would be bound also in heaven. That is to say: Whoever in His Church did not believe that his sins were forgiven him, they were not forgiven, but whoever believed and turned aside from them by repentance, having placed himself in the bosom of the Church, would be healed by the same faith and repentance.[28]

How was this instrumentation effected, practically, in the life of the church? The chief means was through penance. Penance, for Augustine, was closely related to the nature of sin and was clearly for purposes of helping the sinner. " We should not despair of God's mercy in the matter of forgiving in the Holy Church every crime . . . if we do penance each according to the measure of his sin." Thus, penance was intimately related to the sin. " In doing of penance, when the sin is such as to separate the sinner even from the body of Christ, it is not so much the length of the penance that we should take account of as the sorrow of the penitent." [29] This is not a legalistic point of view. It does not see penance as a way of atoning for a sin committed. Rather, in emphasizing, not length of time so much as the dimension of depth, Augustine has described penance as a means — an instrumentation — by which forgiveness is made real. It is for this reason that, within the church, seasons of penance should be appointed. For inner feelings do "not come to the notice of others, although it is manifest to Him." [30] By providing for the seasons of penance, the church provides the opportunity in which the instrumentation of forgiveness can be real to each person.

At the heart of penance is almsgiving. The greatest form of almsgiving is forgiveness of others who have wronged one. "For to forgive a man who seeks pardon is itself a giving of alms. And accordingly, our Lord's saying 'Give alms, and behold all things are clean to you' applies to every useful act of mercy." Therefore, from awareness of the need for an instrument of forgiveness in his own conversion, from the sense that the instrument existed within the church, Augustine moved to the understanding that penance within the church was the particular instrument. It is surely no accident that these last statements came from that time when he was Bishop of Hippo and thus, as a pastor, was concerned with helping others make real what had become real to him.

In conclusion, two summary observations about Augustine's view of forgiveness are in order. One is that Augustine must have been aware that possible danger lay in centering too much on the instrumentality of forgiveness. When he said that the church on earth stands through the forgiveness of sins,[31] he was saying that there was a sense in which the church mediates the context of forgiveness. It is not just an instrument. On the contrary, to see just the instrumental is to lead to idolatry and not to "realized forgiveness." For Augustine asked, "How, then, could all things be clean for the Pharisees, even though they give alms and yet are not believers." [32] He answered his own question by saying, "Surely those who live in great wickedness and take no pains to correct their life and moral habits, though amid all their crimes and misdeeds they incessantly multiply almsgiving, yet all in vain do they take comfort to themselves from our Lord's saying: 'Give alms; and behold, all things are clean to you.'" [33] That is to say, the instrumentation of forgiveness, without the context of forgiveness, is to no avail in the total experience of forgiveness.

On the contrary, Augustine elsewhere wrote: " He who produces or worships any symbol, unaware of what it means, is enslaved to a sign." [34] In other words, to see a sign, including the sign of almsgiving, apart from the context, is not to be free but is to be bound. Such binding is idolatry.

Thus, Augustine contributed greatly to our understanding of the instrumental side of forgiveness. He formulated what needed to be formulated in his time. Also, he *almost* prophesied the dangers of his position if pushed too far. These are dangers that have indeed been fulfilled in the churches — Protestant and Roman Catholic — of the Western world.

The other observation, therefore, is that although Augustine indicated the dangers of identifying forgiveness with the instrumentation alone, yet one wonders if he fully saw them. I said he " almost " prophesied the future, because he himself began to assign more to the nature of instrumentality than was its warrant. In Chapter 19 of his Enchiridion, he said: " Our life must be changed for the better and alms must be used in propitiating God for past sins." Farther along in the same paragraph we read these words: " This prayer [the Lord's Prayer] completely washes away very small sins of daily life. It also washes away those sins which once made the life of the believer very wicked, but which, through penance, changed for the better, he has given up." [35]

To say that penance in any form actually washes away the sin is contrary to the insights gained both from Scripture and from parish research. The act cannot be undone; it is the effect of sin that is removed. That these last-quoted statements do not fit consistently with the rest of his comments on forgiveness is a demonstration of what happens both to faith and practice when the full dimension of forgiveness is not recognized. It is the same danger that befalls today's pastor when, desiring to be effective, he uses gimmicks in his preaching or substitutes the techniques of counseling for the practice of shepherding.

From this experience in the West, let us now turn to the East. Even today, one way to describe the difference between West and East is to say that the one is systematic and literal, whereas the other is symbolic and pictorial. Whereas art in the West tended to become literal in the representation of what it said (until modern art), that in the East was only suggestive. The language of the East, such as Hebrew, is a picture language. As a result, in the East, emphasis was, and is, much more on the whole picture into which details are to be placed rather than on the details themselves. This is seen particularly in the difference between church liturgy in the East and that in the West. Today, the whole mood of Western worship is a means to an end. It is something that is done as a representation of a specific theological position. Hence, behind the liturgy of the Baptist churches is their theology of Baptism. Behind the liturgy of the pulpit-centered church is a theology of the Word. Behind the liturgy of the altar-centered church is a theology of the Sacrament. By contrast, in the Eastern church, the liturgy *is* the theology. The liturgy is the whole picture that encompasses the details; it is not a detail that gives expression to the picture. In short, the Eastern emphasis is upon the context in which life is lived.

Therefore, with the Eastern fathers of the early church, thought seemed to develop in terms of passion, of intellect, and of the symbol of light. It is not that those of the West did not speak of light or have passion and intellect; but these three terms seem to characterize the world of the East in a way that is different from the West. The East seemed to have a greater emphasis on asceticism than the West. It seemed concerned with that which would enable men to be rid of the details — the instruments — of life and allow for concentration on the context. There seemed to be an emphasis on mysticism and imitation rather than on obedience.

There were several great personalities who reflected this dimension. Although Athanasius is the one on whom to concentrate as a parallel to Augustine, it is well to understand him by seeing him within the context of Clement of Alexandria, Origen, and Dionysius the Areopagite.

Clement of Alexandria, who died ca. A.D. 225, was the founder of an important school. He lived about the end of the time in which the Shepherd of Hermas was significant. As the Shepherd represented a response to the concern for instrumentality, Clement represented that development which showed concern for the context. If forgiveness is seen as the context in which we live, and it is a proclaimed context, then the important thing is to contemplate that forgiveness and to imitate it. The focus of contemplation, of course, is God — but God in Jesus Christ. This is why a school was important to Clement. His school was a place of contemplation.

Along with the idea of instruction and contemplation came the word " light." Clement thought that man was called *phōs* (light) by the ancients. He wrote:

As, then, those who have shaken off sleep forthwith become all awake within, or rather, as those who try to remove a film that is over the eyes, do not supply to them from without the light which they do not possess, but removing the obstacles from the eyes, leave the pupil free; then also we who are baptized, having wiped off the sin which obscures the light of the Divine Spirit, have the eye of the spirit free, unimpeded, and full of light, by which alone we contemplate the Divine, the Holy Spirit flowing down to us from above.[36]

Clement is speaking here of the dynamic experience of freedom. He identifies lack of freedom with sin. Hence, although he does not use the word " forgiveness," he is speaking of the same experience that we identify as " realized forgiveness." He identifies this experience, however, not with the means or instrument, but with the context, with the very light itself. For " the darkness is ignorance through which we fall into sin. . . . Knowledge is the illumination we receive which makes ignorance disappear and endows us with clear vision." [37] Again he says: " Do you not hear that we are no longer under the law, but under the master of free choice." [38]

Just as Augustine centered on the instrumentation but did not ignore the matter of the context, so Clement, in centering upon the context, did not ignore the matter of the instrumentation. Clement referred to Jesus' speaking of eating his flesh and drinking his blood as describing " distinctly by metaphor the drinkable properties of faith and the promise, by means of which the church . . . is welded together." [39] Instruction is the means by which we make the light real, and that is the function of the church. He suggested that the church should be called after the concept of the Virgin for the reason that we are nurtured by the church and nurture is the mothering or female function.[40] Yet, even here, it was the context that was important. For the instructor was Jesus, and it was out of salvation that instruction came, not the reverse.[41]

In the thought of Origen, the motif of Clement was developed and expanded. Origen was a student at Alexandria. There were two phases in his life, but the Eastern mood dominated. Origen was aware of asceticism, intellect, and the experience of contemplation. Origen emphasized the use of the mind, and the completeness and wholeness of things — i.e., the contextual dimension. Hence he said in *De Principiis* that the apostles had stated very clearly what should be believed, but that they had left it for others to determine the grounds of their statements and to investigate them under the Holy Spirit — to " those persons, I mean, who should prepare themselves to be fit and worthy receivers of wisdom." [42]

The danger of the emphasis on the context within the totality of forgiveness is that, in the course of time, the step is made into a land where guilt is not important at all. Illumination becomes everything. It is the light that makes the difference. In the fifth-century writings assigned to one called Dionysius the Areopagite, this is what happened. One commentator wrote of him: " In the celestial world of Dionysius we are removed from the preoccupations of St. Paul; we are no longer in a world where guilt has any place." [43]

It is not by its worst but by its best, however, that the position of the East should be understood. Athanasius, with his concern for integrity and wholeness is an example of the best. Athanasius stood much in the East as Augustine did in the West. Although he lived a little earlier than Augustine, their dates overlap. Like Augustine, Athanasius was a man of considerable scholarship. Both men were influenced by the example of the monastics — particularly Antony. Whereas Augustine was a central figure leading to the future of the church in the West, Athanasius was a central figure behind one of the most important councils in the history of the church — Nicaea. Athanasius' life pattern was different from Augustine's in that it was not one of moving in and out of doubt. However, he did move in and out of exile in accord with the winds of politics. Supremely important, Athanasius was a pastor and church administrator. The article on him in the *Encyclopedia of Religion and Ethics* says: " Athanasius, though an Alexandrian, was not a speculative theologian, but . . . a great Christian pastor. . . . Arianism was to his pastoral mind not heterodoxy, but impiety and soul-destroying." [44] It is out of this pastoral concern for people to be whole, or saved, that Athanasius is to be understood.

The general approach of Athanasius was that of return to the gospel, not just speculation. He lived during a time when much of the speculation centered on the idea of God.[45] For him, the issue was not so much one of speculative belief, but of worship and relationship. The need for redemption was basic in his thinking, but it was not expressed in terms of forgiveness as much as in terms of sin, knowledge, and light. Hence, like Clement and Origen before him, his concern was forgiveness understood as a context.

His treatise *On the Incarnation of the Word* reveals that Athanasius was concerned with the same basic dynamic that is here described as " realized forgiveness." According to Athanasius, God is known by what he does — specifically by creation.[46] However, man by his sin cannot see God in creation. " Consistently, therefore, the Word of God took a body and has made use of a human instrument in order to quicken the body also, and as He is known in creation . . . to shew himself everywhere, leaving nothing void of His own divinity and of the knowledge before Him." [47] In this statement, there is the context of the presence of God. There is the instrumentation of the cross. There is the resultant new awareness of creation.

As with Clement, so with Athanasius the word " light " is important. The light expresses the contextual nature of forgiveness. In his book *The Light of the World,* Jaroslav Pelikan has developed the place of this concept in the thought of Athanasius. Pelikan calls attention to the significance of Ps. 36:9 for Athanasius when it says, " In thy light do we see light." Beginning with a word from Athanasius, Pelikan writes:

" Salvation proceeds from the Saviour, just as illumination does from the light." Wherever Athanasius spoke of illumination, he meant some aspect of salvation; and wherever his language turned to the images of salvation and of cleansing, the image of illumination helped to clarify what those images implied.[48]

The light frees man from the darkness. This light also mediates the context of forgiveness. " For like as He is the Father's Word and Wisdom, so too condescending to created things, He becomes, to impart the knowledge and apprehension of Him that begat Him." [49] And again, in his *Discourse I Against the Arians*, Athanasius wrote that " there was need of God; and the Word of God; that those who had become under a curse, He himself might set free." [50] That is to say, the context of God was needed and necessary to make men free.

With regard to the need for an instrumentation of that which makes men free, Athanasius made several references. Again, in his work *On the Incarnation of the Word* he wrote:

Much more did God the Word of the all-good Father not neglect the race of men, His work, going to corruption: but, while He blotted out the death which had ensued by the offering of His own body, He corrected their neglect by His own teaching, restoring all that was man's by His own power.[51]

However, in his biographical sketch of the life of Antony, Athanasius shows that in practice, he is far more aware of the context of forgiveness than of the instrumentation. This is precisely the reverse of the situation that was seen with Augustine; for there are features that stand out in the conversion of Antony as told by Athanasius. He emphasizes that Antony was in the context of good men and of the discipline of the context of forgiveness. " He subjected himself in sincerity to the good men whom he visited, and learned thoroughly where each surpassed him in zeal and discipline." [52] This is not the type of discipline that is after the manner of penance. It is not a matter of making forgiveness real by paying for what has been done wrong — as in the Western approach. Instead, this is the discipline of becoming a part of the context, of the given of God. " He took note of the piety towards Christ and the mutual love which animated all. . . . With others of the same age he had no rivalry; save this only, that he should not be second to them in higher things." [53]

In matter of fact, the instrumentation to which Athanasius

pointed was, consistent with the Eastern view, the instrumentation of contemplation. About contemplation, he quotes Antony as saying: " There is need of much prayer and of discipline that when a man has received through the Spirit the gift of discerning spirits, he may have power to recognise their characteristic." [54] Therefore, Athanasius reports that, as a matter of custom, Antony would return to his cell and discipline himself to the " thought of the mansions in heaven, having his desire fixed on them, and pondering over the shortness of man's life." [55] The purpose of all this was that, by ordering the life daily, " we shall neither fall into sin, nor have a lust for anything, nor cherish wrath against any, nor shall we heap up treasure upon earth." [56]

Does Athanasius then have no place for penance or repentance? He does, but not in the same sense as that found in the West. In a pastoral letter for Easter, he concluded his message by saying:

Let those of us who are far off return, confessing our iniquities, and having nothing against any man, but by the spirit mortifying the deeds of the body. For thus, having first nourished the soul here, we shall partake with angels at that heavenly and spiritual table.[57]

Thus, there is a place for repentance; but the things one does are not to destroy bondage to sin, but to place one in the context of forgiveness.

VI THE SPLIT THROUGHOUT HISTORY

This typology has its counterparts throughout the rest of history. In the world it can be seen in the continuing difference between the church of the East and the church of the West. It can also be seen in the history of the Western church itself. There has been the emphasis of the mystics and the pietists. A case in point is found in the words of Thomas à Kempis in *The Imitation of Christ:* If one would lead a devout life, let his gaze be fixed wholly on Jesus Christ. On the other side there have been the great systems of thought built by such men as Thomas Aquinas, Luther, and Calvin.

Of particular interest in this second half of the twentieth century is the fact that these two camps can also be seen in the current approaches to personality. Sigmund Freud symbolizes the

West. His approach is highly aware of the need for structure. His view of the id takes cognizance of powerful forces within man. Some of these are forces of love (eros) and some of them are forces of hate (thanatos). Man has to come to terms with these forces in order to be free of them. If he succeeds, he is " saved," and if he fails he is neurotic — i.e., he sins. In order to come to terms with these forces, Freud suggests the place of the father figure. The father figure for each individual is the one in whose presence the freedom is worked out. It is never that the sin of the past is done away; it is that the father helps find the instrumentation whereby the effect of the sin can be covered or the weight lifted.

The other camp is symbolized by Carl Rogers. If Freud's view is Western and characterized by a sense of the negative or the demonic in man, Rogers' position is Eastern and characterized by the phrase " Know thyself." Although aware of powerful forces within the personality, Dr. Rogers holds that these are basically forces for good. The personality, he would say, has tremendous capabilities if experiences can be brought into the awareness and there dealt with. This happens when there is a proper context. " Acceptance," not " agreement," is the central word in the dictionary of client-centered therapy. In the framework of Clement, it is not the father that is the prime figure but the mother. We need that which will always accept us as we are, though we are unacceptable, and nurture us. In Freud's view, there is a place for revolt against the father figure in the Oedipus Complex; but there is no place for revolt in Rogers' — just disintegration because of lack of awareness.

The Bible and the early church have been put together, next to the experiences in modern pastoral care, because both say something to the split in the current approach to personality. They say that out of pastoral theology and its key word " realized forgiveness," we learn that both camps are needed. The word that the church has to say to all who deal with human personality is the same word that was written in the so-called Second Letter of Clement:

And the Church, being spiritual, was revealed in the flesh of Christ, showing us that if any guard her in the flesh and do not corrupt her, he shall receive her again in the Holy Spirit. For this flesh is the anti-type of the Spirit; no one, accordingly, who has corrupted the antitype shall receive the reality. So, then, brother, it means this: Guard the flesh, so that you may share in the Spirit.[58]

Thus, Clement says that that is needed which is both context and instrument — spirit and flesh. Destroy the one, and you destroy the other. For the realization of forgiveness, we need both the structure provided by the symbol of the Freudian father and the context provided by the symbol of the Rogerian mother.

VII NEW ELEMENTS IN RELATION TO FORGIVENESS

Whether we are speaking in terms of the East or of the West, three new elements emerge with regard to forgiveness that were not seen in the Bible.

To begin with, forgiveness was seen more as something for the next world than for the present. Augustine said, " Now the forgiveness of sins has reference chiefly to the future judgment." [59] In the light of the persecutions of his time, this is understandable. Harnack observes that Origen and Tertullian considered it vain to celebrate birthdays. Since it is forgiveness in the next world that is important, it is the death date that should be noted.[60] However, consistent with the Biblical view of time and newness, the future was not unrelated to the present. In the early church, there was a different view of space and time than just that of unending days. For the future God, said Harnack, was present, and the preaching of the future was also in the present. Thus, as the Letter of Barnabas taught, when we receive forgiveness of sins, we are renewed and " God truly dwells in us as in his habitation." [61] Such a statement is a different understanding of space from that of just three dimensions.

The second new element is that the church as the context of forgiveness and the church as the instrument of forgiveness have become more intimately related than before. This was done in the Shepherd of Hermas through the symbol of a tower. The tower is the context in which forgiveness can be found, and it is also the instrument that makes it real.

That the church is related to the covenant — i.e., the context of forgiveness — is continually emphasized. Hence, Barnabas said that

God gave the covenant, but that the people were not worthy because of their sin. Thus, by suffering on our account, Christ mediated to us this context of forgiveness which is the covenant.[62] The church was before all ages as the body of Christ, we are told by Clement.[63] And in the Second Letter of Clement, we are informed that by doing the will of God, we shall belong to this covenant of forgiveness.[64] The particular lesson of this for the understanding of forgiveness is realization that the *covenant nature of forgiveness as a context has continuity* to it. In relation to the new insight about time, this means that in the church, forgiveness as a context is related to the past as well as the future and unites both in a given moment of experience.

The instrumental dimension of the church is seen in both East and West. It is seen in the practice of making pilgrimages to relics after the manner of Gregory of Nyssa [65] or following the specific program of repentance as outlined by Tertullian.[66] Tertullian was the first to speak of the church as the " arch of salvation." The need to take seriously the instrumentality of forgiveness as related to the church is one of his major contributions.

The third insight centered on the matter of second repentance. This was the difference between relation to the context of forgiveness and relation to the instrumentation. It was particularly expressed in the Shepherd of Hermas.

VIII   CONCLUSION

Two fundamental insights from the Scripture are confirmed and upheld during this period of the early church:

1. The necessity for forgiveness as a realized experience is established again and again. When forgiveness as a reality fails, the result is either heresy or reformation. By the fifth century, the practice of penance in the West was becoming very lax. According to McNeill, the result was a growing interest in monasticism. The experience of Tertullian himself is an example. When he centered on one dimension of forgiveness, it was not sufficient. He therefore centered on the other dimension. The result was heresy. On the other hand, in the East, when people began just to intellectualize, the same problem arose. Athanasius is an example of one who resisted this danger, and Dionysius the Areopagite

one who gave in. Insofar as the church was an agent for "realized forgiveness," it was genuinely relevant. When the church failed, the result was intellectualizing, polytheism, and similar escapes to try to make up for a basic lack.

2. A look at the early church also confirms that there is realization of forgiveness, but only when the world of dimensions (instruments) is united with the world of no dimensions (a context) does it happen. Only in Christ, or a fellowship that becomes the body of Christ, are forgiveness as a context and forgiveness as an instrument brought together in a field of experience that allows one the freedom to be newly creative.

The attempts to make the church this agent of unity were expressed in confession before the whole church, in martyrdom, exorcism, the Sacrament, penance, and contemplation. Regardless of which agents were found, the real gift of the Christian faith is that it points to the spiritual awareness and the resurrection of the body that makes forgiveness real. Idolatry tries to make forgiveness real by using only three dimensions, and it fails. Gnosticism tried to do it by ignoring the world of dimensions and centering on the world of no dimensions. Only the Christian faith brings the two worlds together.

5

Forgiveness in Search of Reality

I INTRODUCTION

THIS chapter is not a history of the cure of souls nor of the experience of forgiveness. Those who are interested in such a history should study the excellent works of John T. McNeill. Rather, this chapter is an overview to sense the sweep of Western history with regard to forgiveness, to take note of the degree to which "realized forgiveness" played a part in the thinking of the Reformation, and to understand the framework of today's understanding of forgiveness.

At the beginning of the previous chapter, it was said that all history could be written as a search for forgiveness. In the Western church this history would be written as the history of reaction to, or refinement of, the instrumentation of forgiveness. Just as the history of the Eastern church has been seen in the contextual understanding of forgiveness, yet not without a degree of instrumentation, so the Western emphasis on the instrumentation has not been totally unaware of the need for the contextual dimension. Yet from the fall of Rome to the present day, the instrumentation of forgiveness has been the central feature of Western Christianity.

This is first observed in the Celtic penitentials. Penitentials were books that advised the priests as to the type of penance that should be given for various types of sin. The penitential was perhaps the most practical and admitted tool for the instrumentation of forgiveness ever devised. The emphasis on instrumentation is seen also in those studies which show the development of the liturgy in the years after Gregory the Great. Parts were added to the ritual to meet the needs of time and culture — that is, to make the service real — without much thought of the total picture of the service. At some points, the liturgy seemed as grotesque as a house to which rooms were just added.

Reaction against this extreme emphasis on instrumentation, yet mixed with the desire to keep this pole of the forgiveness experience, developed clearly. There were outcroppings of this reaction in parts of the Franciscan order and later in the Jansenist movement. The Reformation, however, was the major example. Calvin expressed this desire for both context and instrument when he wrote to Farel:

Consider how wretched would be the state and condition of the church if she could be compelled to receive to the partaking in so great a mystery those of whom she is altogether ignorant or perhaps regards with suspicion. And to say nothing of the church, how shall the minister discharge this onerous duty, unless he proceeds upon some fixed and certain methods for separating the worthy from the unworthy communicants.[1]

The first part of this statement expresses the concern for the context. It speaks of the need for the purity of the church. Concern for the instrumentation of forgiveness is shown in the necessity for some method of determining who can receive the Sacrament. In Chapter 2 of this book, research showed that the instrument has to be adequate for the particular person. Not any instrument at any time will do. Here, Calvin is asking for that which will make the church an adequate instrument.

In two ways, the Reformation failed. It failed to reform the Roman Catholic Church. Instead, the Reformation leaders had to leave the Roman Catholic Church or were excommunicated. The Council of Trent was both a response and a reaction to the Reformation. As a response, it did seek to " clean up the mess in Washington," as it were. As a reaction, the Council became just a further crystallization of the instrumental dimension of forgiveness. With its anathemas, the Council made it clear who was and was not in the church and provided the method that defined who was and was not forgiven.

The Reformation failed not only because it did not reform the Roman Church, but also because it produced other churches with the same basic sin against which it had reacted — that of centering upon the instrumental pole and not the total experience of forgiveness. The evangelical thought of the Reformation began to be crystallized in the Councils of Dort and Westminster, and even Heidelberg. Liturgy became crystallized and certain forms were considered Lutheran or Episcopalian, Presbyterian or Baptist. Perhaps worst of all, a church was called by the name of one of its leaders, Luther. That was something Luther had hoped would never happen.

The evidence of this failure in the Reformation is seen in part by those antiorganization groups which expressed themselves in the pietistic movements. The Quaker George Fox sounded like one of the Eastern church fathers when he spoke of the Light and said that " all was manifest and seen in the Light." His contextual emphasis is further expressed in his Journal where he wrote:

The law of God takes hold upon the law of sin and death; but the law of faith, or the law of the Spirit of life, which is the love of God, and which comes by Jesus . . . , this makes free from the law of sin and death. . . . Therefore, ye, who know the love of God, and the law of his Spirit, and the freedom that is in Jesus Christ, stand fast in him . . . and be not entangled with the yoke of bondage." [2]

And again: " None can be a minister of Christ Jesus but in the eternal spirit." [3] To George Fox, a person stood in the context of sin or the context of the Light. Forgiveness was identified with the experience of the context.

However, the thrust of his position never carried the day in the mainstream of Western thought. The position is still much in evidence, but in the seventeenth and eighteenth centuries there were only outcroppings of it in men like John Bunyan and Jonathan Edwards.

Yet, in the nineteenth century and the early part of the twentieth, the weaknesses of a sheer instrumental approach became so clear, and the historical development of scientific method became so pointed a challenge to the superstitious nature of the instrumental approach, that the contextual point of view took the center of the stage. That upstaging was represented in the leaders of modern theology, Friedrich Schleiermacher and Albrecht

Ritschl, in the nineteenth century, and in the social gospel of the present century.

The preparation for the present century was the compartmentalization of man's mind. Since the Reformation, there had been a growing wall between theology, on one side, and life and science on the other. It was known that man had three lobes to his brain, and that they symbolically housed life, knowledge, and religion. It was forgotten that these three were in one person. The present century has seen an attempt to end this compartmentalization. Philosophically, the attempt is seen in Whitehead and his statement that all truth is one. Scientifically, it is seen in Einstein and his search for a unified field theory. Theologically, it is seen in Barth, Bultmann, Berdyaev, and Tillich — each of whom has sought to present wholistic approaches to faith and life.

II   THE EARLY CHURCH TO THE REFORMATION

The problem of the Reformation is symbolized in Thomas Aquinas. In the thirteenth century, he gave the church the instrumentation of a great structure of theology. That instrumentation included his blessing on penance as a sacrament. The greatness of his structure lay in the fact that it provided a unity in which all things held together. This included the relation of the pope and the ecclesiastical structure to the instrumentation of forgiveness. That against which the Reformers reacted was centered largely in Saint Thomas and many of those practices which were a logical outgrowth of his system.

However, Thomas Aquinas did not just happen. He did not create his system out of nothing. The work of this master scholar represented the pulling together of thought, practice, and activity. John T. McNeill, in *A History of the Cure of Souls,* expresses the situation of the thirteenth century in this way:

By the thirteenth century a type of penitential discipline had come to prevail in the Western Church which was widely different from that of the Patristic Age. Instead of being public and unusual, confession and penance had become private, frequent and common to all. Whereas in the early period the offender was hesitantly admitted to one, or possibly a second, act of penance, every Christian was now under obligation to come to penance not less than once a year. The ancient exomologesis was no longer in use, and confession was made under seal of absolute secrecy. Formerly a public reconciliation normally followed the assigned period of penance: absolution was now commonly accorded in private when the penance was undertaken. The discipline was embraced within the sacramental system of the medieval Church, and priests rather than bishops were its principal administrators.[4]

Although tradition has ascribed the start of this development to others in the fifth and sixth centuries, the earliest penitential is by Saint Finnian of Clonard, who died about the middle of the sixth century.[5] The basic principle that governed this penitential was the principle of the contraries. The theory was that a fault was best cured by the contrary to it. If a man was too involved in sex, the cure was total abstinence — even from his wife. This thought of equating the act of penance with the type of sinful deed became basic. It was a logical outgrowth of Augustine's view. Thus, the Irish Penitential of Columban at the beginning of the seventh century required of monks that:

The talkative person is to be sentenced to silence, the disturber to gentleness, the gluttonous to fasting, the sleepy fellow to watchfulness, the proud to imprisonment, the deserter to expulsion; everyone shall suffer suitable penalties according to what he deserves, that the righteous may live righteously.[6]

And of laymen as well as clergymen, the instructions continued:

Diversity of guilt occasions diversity of penalty; for even the physicians of bodies prepare their medicines in various sorts. For they treat wounds in one way, fevers in another, swellings in another. . . . So therefore the spiritual physician ought also to heal with various sorts of treatment.[7]

This procedure led then to the classification of sins and the type of penance that was required for each. It was not unlike those booklets from Unity, and similar groups today, that identify a sin with each disease and a type of prayer for each sin.

What happened in the presentation of these penitentials was simply that the procedures of the ancient disciplines had been changed or replaced. In the typology of this book, however, the penitentials were still instrumentalities and not of the context of forgiveness. Their major significance lay in their forming the transition from public confession and penance to the private and sacramental practice of the thirteenth century. In so doing, they removed almost all practical sense of the context of the church and of forgiveness, and they centered upon the instrumentation pole. According to McNeill, there was tremendous pressure for this private approach. It had precedent in the practice of medical doctors. It was easier. It was popular. It became the law and the practice in the end of the seventh century when the Penitential of Theodore (Archbishop of Canterbury) said: " Reconciliation is not publicly established in the province, for the reason that there is no public penance either." [8]

Despite the pressure, however, the change was neither universal nor speedy. As the secular religious orders were later to have trouble being accepted by the regular clergy, so the penitentials also did not receive immediate acceptance. The episcopate had its doubts — some administrative and some personal. Both types of doubt were understandable. From an administrative standpoint, there were many variations in the different codes. The high degree of difference from one to another gave rise to a skeptical look. Further, the practice developed of getting substitutes to do one's penitential acts.[9] An eighth-century Irish table of commutations began:

The *arreum* for saving a soul out of hell, viz. 365 paternosters and 365 genuflexions and 365 blows with a scourge on every day to the end of a year, and fasting every month saves a soul out of hell. For this *arreum* for redeeming the soul that deserves torments in the body has been made according to the number of joints and sinews that are in a man's body.[10]

In the minds of some, this approach was questionable. Such a program of substitution was not initially accepted.

The personal objection of bishops to these programs lay in the matter of jurisdiction. The penitential practices were not under ecclesiastical authority. On that point, one may suspect that the bishops had a vested interest of concern; but it is an understandable interest. Lack of order meant also lack of effective instrumentation of the church in the area of forgiveness.

However, the demand of the populace won. In many respects, though physically severe, the private penance was emotionally easier than the public. It freed the penitent from the humiliation of public rebuke.

Private penance had several results. It tended to reduce the dimensions of " realized forgiveness " to one. It eliminated what previously has been designated as essential for the experience of forgiveness — the context. The increased privacy pulled the penitent away from the sense of the context. Since forgiveness demands a context, this made it emotionally necessary for the establishment of the idea that the clergy were the real church. This double standard of clergy and laity was necessary the minute that penance and absolution became private in the sense that the penitentials made them.

The shift also tended to reduce the dynamic nature of the instrument of penance itself. It will be recalled from Chapter 2 that the value of the instrument is that it helps make the forgiveness real. Here, the acts of penance actually became forms of punishment — a paying of a fine. This mechanical approach was like treating a modern neurosis with an aspirin. It dealt with the symptom of a problem. The more that people sought an instrument and made the instrument the most important aspect of forgiveness, the farther they moved from that which could make forgiveness real.

Yet the people of those middle ages were in search of the same dynamic experience that I have earlier identified with the experience of forgiveness. The prayers used to confer God's forgiveness upon the penitent demonstrate the point. The note of freedom is expressed in one prayer where the priest asked that " just as none of us is free from guilt, so none may be a stranger to pardon." [11] And again, " have mercy on those who have confessed, that what is bound by the chain of things accursed, the greatness of thy love may release." [12]

A ninth-century Frankish prayer also shows how the desire for " realized forgiveness " was expressed in the culture of the day. It shows fear for life after death and the torments of hell, a keen awareness of relationship with others, and knowledge of the means (instruments) of grace in the church.

I beseech, O Lord, the majesty of Thy kindness and mercy that Thou wilt deign to accord pardon to this Thy servant as he confesses his sins and evil deeds, and remit the guilt of his past offenses — Thou who did'st carry back the lost sheep upon Thy shoulders and did'st hearken with approval to the prayers of the publican when he confessed. Wilt Thou also, O Lord, deal graciously with this Thy servant; be Thou favorable to his prayers, that he may abide in the grace of confession, that his weeping and supplication may quickly obtain Thy enduring mercy, and, readmitted to the holy altars and sacraments, may he again be made a partaker in the hope of eternal life and heavenly glory. Through our Lord Jesus Christ.[13]

The early part of this prayer indicates a sense of freedom by virtue of the lifting of the weight of guilt. The middle part seems to suggest a sense of the context of forgiveness when it asks " that he may abide in the grace of confession." However, this notion is quickly ended when the prayer moves on to ask " that his weeping and supplication may quickly obtain Thy enduring mercy." In other words, confession was understood not in relation to a context but as a means of persevering in the instrumental dimension of forgiveness. As has been stated, such perseverance always reduces the instrument to a matter of works and to the idolatry that is worship of works. With the contextual dimension, the sacrament can well be an instrument that makes real one's forgiveness. However, without a prior sense of the context of forgiveness, the sacrament is not adequate.

By the time of the Reformation, the sacramental aspect of penance had reached a level wherein the relation between penance and the worship of the church had been severed. The emphasis was not so much on penance *and* worship as a means of making forgiveness real, as on penance alone as a means of keeping the soul out of hell. A priest might designate worship as a part of the penitential act. Yet worship as a penalty, and worship as an experience of the presence of God, are two different things. There was not the close relation between confession and the Mass that was reflected in the shift-of-feeling tests given to Roman Catholics and described in Chapter 2.

III   FORGIVENESS IN THE REFORMERS

From the preceding discussion, it is not at all surprising to find the sixteenth century described as an age of guilt and fear. In the case of some people, such guilt and fear led to the almost wild use of indulgences. The fear was of eternity and of not having the fruit of forgiveness — peace. In the case of other people, particularly Martin Luther, this led to a tireless search. He tried beatings and pilgrimages. He used all the instruments that could be devised.

The tragedy was that the Western interest in structure had allowed a means to become an end. Indulgences became important in and of themselves. Piety was measured not by a life but by the number of penitential acts a person had to his credit. Like the child who has never missed Sunday school, virtue was measured by the number of perfect attendance bars. The church of salvation had come to be seen as the expression of man's search for God, not God's love of man.

In this situation, many men were beginning to look for an answer. Zwingli, Bucer, Farel, Knox, the Waldensians, and a host of others could be mentioned. Later, the names of Wesley, Zinzendorf, Fox, Freylinghausen, and Tennent could be added. Yet, when thought is given to the Reformation, two names invariably stand out as central. One is Luther. He was the man of passion tempered by intellect. A student, a lawyer, an Augustinian priest, a tract writer, a man of insight and moods, he was unquestionably the emotional center of the Reformation. The other man is Calvin. If Luther was a man of passion tempered with intellect, Calvin was a man of intellect tempered with love. The latter point is debated, if it is considered at all, by most people. The austerity of Calvin's theocracy, the decision on the death of Servetus, and the rigor of his theology create this image.

Nevertheless, if the significance of the Reformation in relation to the realization of forgiveness is to be understood, these two men must be seen as persons. Like Luther, Calvin too was a scholar and a lawyer. Is it not strange that Calvin, with his French background, should be seen as the one who is austere, and Luther, the German, should be considered the man who was warm? The love in Calvin is not found in his formal theological writings, but in his letters. There the reader discovers a man who was afflicted all his life with infected gums. There one senses a compassion as he speaks of or writes to his wife, his friends in England, Bucer (a man with whom he had some deep disagreements), and Melanchthon. Calvin had intellect tempered with love; but many do not take the time to see it.

The great contribution of these men to the recovery of forgiveness as a realized experience was a deep awareness of the corporate nature of life. Each in his own way preceded John Donne's "No man is an island, entire of itself." The fact that forgiveness could not center upon the pole of instrumentation was the opening point of Luther's Ninety-five Theses posted October 31, 1517.

1. Our Lord Jesus Christ when he said "Repent" willed that the whole life of believers should repent.
2. This word cannot be understood as referring to sacramental penance, that is, confession and satisfaction, which is performed in the ministration of priests.[14]

Three contributions were made with regard to the realization of forgiveness by Calvin and Luther. Although these contributions were expressions of a different time, they were reemphases of points found in the Bible and the history of the early church. Both men quoted considerably from the fathers of both East and West. These three contributions centered on the themes of freedom, faith, and the total church.

The subject of freedom was dealt with particularly by Calvin. Calvin's insight with regard to freedom was that man is not free to do what he wills, but free to accept or reject forgiveness. His view that " it is certain that the mind of man is not changed for the better except by God's prevenient grace "[15] shows not only his awareness of the dynamic but also of the contextual side of forgiveness. He then goes on to hold that if a man sins, he sins because he has not accepted forgiveness.[16] What makes freedom free is the ability, within the context of forgiveness, not to accept even forgiveness. Thus, prayer is the freedom to converse with God,[17] and Christ is given us " to free us at once from shame and fear, which might well have thrown our hearts into despair."[18]

In speaking of forgiveness, Luther refers to it as that experience which allows the Holy Spirit to return to us and enliven us.[19] That is, we become new creatures and new creators. What is it that we are able to create? We are able to create forgiveness of our brother. We must do it, says Luther, " that thereby we may prove and give testimony that we from God have received forgiveness of sins." [20] In this statement, Luther shows that forgiveness makes possible the freedom to forgive, and the act of forgiving is the instrument by which the forgiveness of ourselves becomes real. This view is a recovery of the Biblical and pastoral picture of " realized forgiveness."

Particularly in the thought of Luther, faith was the great ingredient in making forgiveness real. Faith could be defined as that personal experience which resulted in action. Virtue did not make a person whole, but faith did. Faith postulated the context of forgiveness, because faith was to desire God's forgiveness and to believe that you had received it. In the thought of Luther, repentance began to take a lesser role, although it certainly was not eliminated. It was faith that was central.[21] Calvin gave perhaps more place to repentance than Luther, but he related the two by saying that faith made repentance possible.

When Luther and Calvin emphasized that forgiveness became real in the total church, they seemed to view the church as both the context and the instrumentation of forgiveness. For Luther, " the forgiveness of sins is declared only in God's Word, and there we must seek it." [22] Where is that Word found? It is found in the church. It is what makes church the church. Therefore, for Luther absolution is the actual preaching of the Word of God.[23] That is the context. But the signs, i.e., the way in which forgiveness is made real, are in the church too. " God has given signs and tokens enough, that our sins shall be forgiven; namely, the preaching of the gospel, baptism, the Lord's Supper, and the Holy Ghost in our hearts." [24] These signs are the instruments of forgiveness.

For Calvin, it was similar. Specifically, Calvin wrote in the *Institutes*, " Not only does the Lord through forgiveness of sins receive and adopt us once for all into the church, but through the same means he preserves and protects us there." [25] Thus, the church is both the context and the means. For him, there was no way to come alive unless the church were considered our mother. " Furthermore, away from her bosom one cannot hope for any forgiveness of sins or any salvation." [26] This context was made real for Calvin, as it was for Luther, in the Sacrament.

Yet, Calvin seems to have described, more systematically than Luther, his understanding of the process by which forgiveness becomes real. As I have elsewhere noted about Calvin:

Forgiveness became real *first* by making restitution for the wrongs that had been done. If someone had sinned against another person, Calvin cited the admonition about leaving one's gift at the altar and first going to square accounts with that person. If the sin was against the church as a whole, the church as a whole had to be asked for forgiveness. It was the church as a whole that showed the forgiveness by admitting the sinner again to the Lord's Supper. If the sin was against God — and fundamentally this meant every sin — repentance before God was needed.

The *second* step in making forgiveness real was genuine " mortification." By " mortification " Calvin meant " sorrow of the mind, and the terror experienced from a knowledge of sin and a sense of the divine judgments." In other words, if forgiveness is ever to be real, a person has to be genuinely aware of needing it and of being sorry for what happened. Calvin had rather picturesque images of what this meant, but they can be attributed to the culture of the time. The important point is that no one can have a real awareness of forgiveness if there is not first real awareness of guilt.

The *third* step in making forgiveness real was " vivication." " Vivication " meant seeing the reality of God's love as clearly as the reality of one's own sin. Practically, this meant that a man should " desire and endeavor to live a holy and pious life, as though it were said that a man dies to himself, that he may begin to live to God." [27]

Calvin and Luther differ not on the reality of instrumentation but on the means. Whereas Luther was most grudging in acknowledging a place for private confession, Calvin saw a place for both public and private confession. Calvin's statement reads:

To impart to us this benefit [forgiveness experienced daily], the keys of the church have been given. When Christ gave the command to the apostles and conferred upon them the power to forgive sins . . . , he did not so much desire that the apostles absolve from sins those who might be converted from ungodliness to the faith of Christ, as that they should perpetually discharge this office among believers. Paul teaches this when he writes that the mission of reconciliation has been entrusted to the ministers of the church and that by it they are repeatedly to exhort the people to be reconciled to God in Christ's name. . . . Therefore, in the communion of saints, our sins are continually forgiven us by the ministry of the church itself when the presbyters or bishops to whom this office has been committed strengthen godly consciences by the gospel promises in the hope of pardon and forgiveness.

This they do both publicly and privately as need requires. For very many, on account of their weakness, need personal consolation. And Paul mentions that not only in public preaching, but from house to house as well, he has attested his faith in Christ, and has individually admonished each man concerning the doctrine of salvation.[28]

This lengthy paragraph not only gives further evidence of the relation between context and instrument in Calvin's thinking, it also shows a two-pronged approach to the instrumental nature itself. Forgiveness is made real corporately through the Sacrament and the fellowship of the whole church. However, it is also made real privately through the individual ministries of the church leadership. The awareness of this dual factor can be seen as an attempt to recognize the value of penance in the realization of forgiveness, but to bring it back to the only place where it can have genuine meaning in connection with forgiveness — viz., the worship of the church. The emphasis on the worshiping congregation in both Calvin and Luther is a basic shift back to a pre-Celtic understanding of the realization of forgiveness.

To conclude this point, note that Calvin holds that " the whole of the gospel is contained under these two headings, repentance and forgiveness of sins " [29] and that " the salvation of his church rests upon these two members alone "; forgiving others as we are already forgiven.[30]

Thus, in the writings of Calvin and Luther, there is a confirmation of the earlier point of view about a contextual and an instrumental polarity in the dynamic that is " realized forgiveness." There is, however, a split in the understanding of the instrumentality. This split is expressed in the question, Which comes first, being forgiven or the ability to forgive?

Calvin's position is supported by the point of view developed in Chapters 2 and 3 of this book. For Calvin, without forgiveness first, it would be impossible even to consider our sin. " For if anyone should question his own conscience, he would be so far from daring intimately to lay aside his cares before God that, unless he relied upon mercy and pardon, he would tremble at every approach." [31] Even though the saints do not always begin prayer with requests for forgiveness, they pray in the context of God's mercy. Calvin cites the example of blood atonement coming before prayer in the Old Testament that made it possible to pray.[32]

Calvin also relates justification to this point. He begins by saying, " The righteousness of faith is reconciliation with God, which consists solely in the forgiveness of sins." [33] This must be so, in Calvin's thought, because the wrath of God rests on all of us so long as all continue to be sinners. His reasoning is that since sin separates man from God, until the restoration of grace through Christ, man can do nothing — not even appreciate what it means for him to say, " I need forgiveness." Therefore, says Calvin:

We add that this is done through forgiveness of sins; for if those whom the Lord has reconciled to himself be judged by works, they will indeed still be found sinners, though they ought, nevertheless, to be freed and cleansed from sin. It is obvious, therefore, that those whom God embraces are made righteous solely by the fact that they are purified when their spots are washed away by forgiveness of sins. Consequently, such righteousness can be called, in a word, " remission of sins." [34]

This means that Calvin sees the context of the forgiveness of sins as that which must come first. Within that context, the instrumentation of forgiveness works in two ways. First it helps to clarify not only the reality but the nature of the sin. Adultery, for example, comes to be seen, not as a sin of breaking a law, but a sin of destroying a personality. As an attack on a personality, it is also an attack on God. Second, the instrumentation works to make real the forgiveness of God. The outgrowth of the first part is a true confession of sin. The outgrowth of the second part is a true confession of faith or act of faith.

In Luther, the picture is quite different. He is clear about the necessity of a context. At one point in his commentary on The Letter to the Hebrews, Luther sounds as though he is saying the same thing as Calvin. Speaking of the apostle's phrase " When he had purged our sins " (Heb. 1:3) , Luther wrote:

By these words he forthwith makes short work of all notions of righteousness and every idea of penances which the natural man holds. It is the supreme mercy of God he commends. This means that it was he who purged our sins and not we ourselves, and that it is our own sins he has purged, and not the sins of somebody else.[35]

In this statement, Luther makes it clear that he is not confusing the context with the instrumentation. Forgiveness does not lie in what man does.

Later, as Luther expounds on Heb. 3:2, " who was faithful to him who made him as also Moses was in all his house," Luther appears to sense the same analogy of dynamics in forgiveness that Calvin does. Luther wrote:

Because of this passage Moses was regarded as approved by God and obtained the highest authority over the people. For the very same reason the Jews set this very man in opposition to Christ, and said, " We know, because it was God himself who spoke to Moses." But on the contrary, this Apostle, in answer to such people, sets Christ, who is indeed not less but more faithful to God. And so Moses and Christ contend with one another as to who is " faithful in the house of God." Still, Moses is but a part of the whole house, namely the head; Christ, however, is not only the head but even its Lord and Founder — as God. Therefore, Christ has an honour greater than Moses in proportion as we regard the house [Christ] as greater than its part (Moses).[36]

Luther here gives a picture of the dynamic process of the realization of forgiveness. There is the mediated context that is recognized in Christ. This indeed is greater than any part — than any instrumentation. Symbolically, Moses represents the law and the instrumentation. Both are part of the house. Elsewhere, there seems to be some basis for this interpretation when Luther states what the pole of instrumentation cannot do. The instrument cannot save. The law alone can contribute only to sin. " Every work of the law done without the grace of God appears good outwardly, but inwardly it is sin."[37] Again he says, " The Law of God, that most wholesome doctrine of life, cannot bring a man to righteousness. It is a hindrance rather than a help."[38]

Yet the import of those statements for the dynamic of forgiveness does not seem to have made an impact on Luther. As a result, not only his approach, but that of Lutheranism through the years (e.g., Martin Marty in our day), has taken a different tack. The suggestion of this shift is indicated in another section of his commentary on Hebrews. Luther reiterated that it was the height of perversity " to hasten to perform good works before God has worked in us, i.e., before we believe." So far, so good.

Upon that he adds, however, " Of course, the natural man shrinks violently from hearing understood in this way, for he must first be reduced to nothing and stand in total darkness before he can hear this Word." [39] Man must believe in the context, i.e., have faith in God, before he can do anything. He must be brought low. Yet what is it that brings him low? Practically speaking, for Luther it is the law — and that is where I find my strong objection to his position.

In " A Brief Explanation of the Ten Commandments, the Creed, and the Lord's Prayer," done in 1520, Luther wrote that the Christian who cannot read the Scripture is required to learn these three items. They contain everything that a Christian needs to know in the Bible or that should be preached or that is necessary for salvation. There are three things a man needs to know in order to be saved. He needs to know: (1) what he ought to do and ought not to do; (2) that he cannot do or leave undone any of these things by his own strength; and (3) that he must know how to find and get this strength. After those statements comes this important paragraph:

When a man is ill, he needs to know first what his illness is — what he can do and what he cannot do. Then he needs to know where to find the remedy that will restore his health and help him to do and leave undone the things he ought. Third, he must ask for this remedy and seek it, and get it or have it brought to him. In like manner, the Commandments teach a man to know illness, so that he feels and sees what he can do and what he cannot do, what he can and what he cannot leave undone, and thus know himself to be a sinner and a wicked man. After that the Creed shows him and teaches him where he may find the remedy — the grace which helps him to become a good man and to keep the Commandments; it shows him God, and the mercy which He has revealed and offered in Christ. In the third place, the Lord's Prayer teaches him how to ask for this grace, get it, and take it to himself, to wit, by habitual, humble, comforting prayer; then grace is given, and by the fulfillment of God's commandments he is saved.[40]

This use of the law is the way a man knows that he is reduced to nothing and stands in total darkness.

If taken seriously, this position of Luther sets a procedure for Christian education and for Christian witness. It is true that salvation and the realization come only within the church and under the grace of God. However, Luther's description of the road from guilt to " realized forgiveness " would be different from Calvin's. With Luther, there first comes the instrumentation of the law which makes one aware that he is living in the context of sin. Next comes the gift of faith. " Faith " is commitment to the context of forgiveness found in Jesus Christ. Finally comes the realization of that forgiveness in the freedom to converse with God through prayer, sacrament, and life. These three parts parallel the three parts of the " Large Catechism " and the three parts of " A Brief Explanation," which are Law, Creed, Prayer. To put this differently, for Luther there is confession of sin, awareness of grace, and confession of, or act of, faith. Thus the first task in education is to teach a man his sin; then show him God's forgiveness.

Now, this difference between Calvin and Luther, and the difference between Luther's position and mine in Chapters 2 and 3, turn out to be more than mere differences of detail. For it is my contention in those earlier chapters that until one is within the context of God's forgiveness, he cannot understand the nature of his sin. It is standing in the presence of Jesus Christ that makes a man aware that he is nothing, and he must say with Peter, " Depart from me, for I am a sinful man, O Lord." The law often made Peter miserable, but Christ alone made him see that he was sinful. In the light of Christ, the law then helped Peter to understand the details and aspects of that sin.

If one asks what a person can do when he is out of this context, an answer must be given. The attractiveness of Luther's position is that it gives a place where the man outside the church can at least start. Yet, if my picture of the dynamics of forgiveness is correct, Luther's error is that life does not work that way. What really happens is that the man outside the church finally becomes dissatisfied with his present existence and begins to seek. Many things may cause this dissatisfaction, including the law, but they are just things. This man may commit himself to liquor, to sex, or to work in an effort to find satisfaction. In response to a witness, he may commit himself to Christ. Then, and only then, will he begin to understand the nature of the life he has led.

The results of the Reformation are still being felt. A trend of thought was recaptured then that continually crops out today in the churches and the thinking of the churches. These outcroppings have not, however, meant peace. As Dr. Telfer has observed, from the Reformation on, the church was really divided over the way in which forgiveness was made real.[41]

Further, the church moved on to crystallize its forms as much as in the past. In the mid-sixteenth century, the Council of Trent met. One of the declarations of the Council stated:

We come at last to satisfaction. Of all the parts of penance, recommended at all times by our Fathers to the Christian people, this has been especially singled out for attack in our day by those who have a semblance of piety but who have disowned its power. With regard to satisfaction the holy Synod declares that it is utterly false and contrary to the word of God that the Lord never forgives the guilt of sin without condoning the entire punishment as well. Not to mention sacred tradition, clear and striking examples are found in the Sacred Scripture to refute plainly this error. . . . Again it is in accord with divine mercy that our sins should not be forgiven without satisfaction, lest we make this a pretext for regarding sin as something trivial. . . . They heal as well the after-effects of sin and by acts of the opposite virtue they remove vicious habits which have been acquired in the course of an evil life.[42]

In this statement, the Celtic principle of contraries was reaffirmed by the Roman Church. Primarily, however, the statement shows that Luther and Calvin were not understood. The emphasis remained on the instrumentation of forgiveness, and the Reformation did not fulfill its objective.

Likewise, the same error began to develop in the churches that grew directly out of the Reformation. The Westminster Assembly in the seventeenth century tried to come to terms with the evangelical position in a structured way. In many places it succeeded, but in many places it did not. Like Saint Thomas, the Divines at Westminster built a huge, unified structure of thought that gave the instrumentation of forgiveness. The hardening of this structure into a form that had to be believed if one was part of the fellowship was a denial of the Reformation.

The result of this hardening left the door open for two trends — both of which were related to the pietistic movements that followed the Reformation. One trend was the expression of individuals who in their own lives and words tried to find a picture of "realized forgiveness." The other was the birth of modern theology in the nineteenth century.

IV   FORGIVENESS IN ECHOES OF THE REFORMATION

So central is man's search for the realization of forgiveness that it cannot die. It may be expressed in different ways, but it will be expressed. Two examples of such expression from the seventeenth and eighteenth centuries are in the writings of Bunyan and Edwards. To them might be added Fox, who was mentioned earlier.

Although there is a sense in which *The Pilgrim's Progress* is a parable of the life of John Bunyan, his real autobiography is found in *Grace Abounding to the Chief of Sinners.* There the reader sees that although Bunyan was neither a drunkard nor a dishonest person in his youth, he was quite devilish. Surely, no one would have confused him with a religious man.[43]

There were, however, a few incidents in his youth that made him think about religion. On one occasion, he was saved from near-drowning. That left him with a sense that he had been saved by God's grace and with a further sense of shame for his laxity in religious matters.[44] The thought later came to him (he remembered it as a voice) that he had a choice of leaving his sins and going to heaven or keeping them and going to hell. Apparently that did not shake him as much as an episode with a woman who had a reputation for swearing. Of all people, *she* rebuked Bunyan for swearing too much. If she thought that he swore in the extreme, Bunyan concluded that he indeed must have been out of line. Thereupon, he met a religious man who started him reading the Bible, and he gave up swearing.

Bunyan observes, however, that this outward change, although it brought many favorable comments, did not really do much to help his inner life. Somehow, although he found the New Testament interesting, he could not fathom Christ. Therefore, he set up as a guide for living, the Ten Commandments. As he later called it in *The Pilgrim's Progress,* he was now living in the "village of Morality." [45]

The real change began when he heard people talk about the

new birth in their lives. He came to feel that he knew Christ and that he could be saved from the law. However, upon reading Luther, the thought crossed Bunyan's mind about Christ, " Let Him go if he will." [46] This thought put Bunyan into a panic, because he felt that he had committed the unpardonable sin. Whereas before, his sins had been against the Mosaic law, now his sin was against the law of the gospel. Bunyan often felt tossed between " the devil and God," as he put it.[47] Yet he finally concluded that two phrases applied to everyone without exception: " Mercy rejoiceth over judgment " and " Him that cometh to me I will in no wise cast out." [48] This experience was followed by Bunyan's feeling a call to the ministry,[49] by his preaching with considerable success, by his imprisonment, and by his writing the epical *Pilgrim's Progress.*

The value of Bunyan's writings is that they demonstrate again not only a concern for forgiveness as central to the gospel and to man's experience but the two polarities that have been the theme of this study. Although it was outside the context of the organized church that he read the law, it was not until he felt himself fully within Christ that the meaning of the sin, and then the meaning of forgiveness, became real. The early instrumentation of that forgiveness was his constant confession of sin. Yet, not until he sensed that he really was within God's mercy could he sense the fullness of his sin which had been against God himself. The later instrumentation of that forgiveness was in his preaching and in his writing *The Pilgrim's Progress.* Both were his confessions and acts of faith. Both were means of making the forgiveness real.

Illustrations need not be multiplied. Sufficient to observe that, in America, Jonathan Edwards sensed the same need to relate the context and the instrumentation of forgiveness. As Dr. John Smith said in editing Edwards' *Religious Affections:* " Edwards never lost sight of the twofold task: on the one hand to defend the central importance of these affections against those who would eliminate them from religion; and on the other, to provide for testing them lest religion degenerate into emotional fanaticism and false enthusiasm." [50]

V FORGIVENESS IN MODERN THEOLOGY

If the two themes of context and instrumentation were to be applied to the West, it might be said that the Roman Catholic Church represented those who were characterized by an emphasis on instrumentation and that the Protestants represented those who were characterized by a search for context — but who never quite made it. To one outside the Roman tradition, it seemed that Catholicism had no concern for the context. The recent Vatican Council demonstrated how false that impression was. Within the Roman Catholic structure, there is a growing and vocal interest in context, but never at the expense of structure. Nevertheless, the dominant motif in Catholicism has been Thomism and the instrumentation that it provides. A discussion of the search for forgiveness within Catholicism, beyond what has been said, must be left to those who are within the structure of that church.

In Protestantism, the impetus for modern theological thought began in Germany. Perhaps America has been too busy covering the frontier to influence the lands from which its people have come. Only in the present century, in one such as Reinhold Niebuhr, has a genuinely American theologian emerged who seems to be casting influence backward to the lands from which America came.

Friedrich Schleiermacher was born after the middle of the eighteenth century and left his influence strongly on the beginning of the nineteenth. He was concerned that theology was intellectually irrelevant and unscientific. The complex and logical systems of theology seemed completely out of touch with the common people. Schleiermacher was unmoved by the intricate discussions as to precisely what a man had to believe to be saved, which view of the atonement a man must hold to be a Christian, or what a man could or could not do. These discussions were no more relevant than the medieval question about the number of angels that could stand on the head of a pin. With regard to developments in scientific and philosophic thought, Schleiermacher had the same problem. The intellectual thinking that was crystallizing the evangelical position seemed to have blind spots where the total sweep of enlightened thought was concerned. Schleiermacher spoke to this latter problem in his famed *On Religion, Speeches to Its Cultured Despisers*. With regard to the first problem — the matter of a faith that was relevant to people — Schleiermacher built upon his *Speeches* and wrote his theological masterpiece, *The Christian Faith*.

For Schleiermacher, the heart of man's need lay in the matter of relationships (particularly to oneself), and the heart of the gospel lay in what it said about man's relationship to God. The first relationship made religion necessary. The second made Christianity the religion that was relevant. Thus, at the opening of *The Christian Faith* he wrote: " The piety which forms the basis of all ecclesiastical communion is considered purely in itself, neither a knowing nor a doing, but a modification of feeling, or of immediate self-consciousness." [51]

This relationship of self-consciousness was not undefined. To Schleiermacher, it was expressed in a feeling of dependence:

The self-consciousness which accompanies all our activity and therefore, since that is never zero, accompanies our whole existence, and negatives absolute freedom, is precisely a consciousness of absolute dependence; for it is the consciousness that the whole of our spontaneous activity comes from a source outside of us in just the same sense in which anything towards which we should have a feeling of absolute freedom must have proceeded from ourselves. But without any feeling of freedom, a feeling of absolute dependence would not be possible.[52]

Within this statement, Schleiermacher made a plea for the contextual dimension of forgiveness. He spoke of the need to be dependent on a source outside ourselves. He spoke of freedom, much as was seen in some of the earlier statements of this book. That is, he saw freedom not as the ability to choose the context, but as freedom only within the context. For him, the feeling of freedom is the way in which the sense of absolute dependence is mediated; without the sense of freedom, " a feeling of absolute dependence would not be possible."

This point of view solved two problems for Schleiermacher. From an intellectual standpoint, it put theology in an area where he could deal with it scientifically. He could also deal with it safely. As the historian has that which defines his area, and the physicist his, so Schleiermacher now had his. From a personal standpoint, Schleiermacher also had brought theology back to where people live. Feelings are relevant to individuals. Relate faith to history or doctrine, and it may seem relevant or it may not. Relate faith to feelings, and everyone finds a point of reference.

Schleiermacher's solution was helpful and pioneering. However, it suffered the fate of all positions that identify the human experience of forgiveness with God himself. Schleiermacher came to identify God with feeling. For him, the two coexisted:

Not only is the feeling of absolute dependence in itself a co-existence of God in the self-consciousness, but the totality of being from which, according to the position of the subject, all determinations of the self-consciousness proceed, is comprehended under that feeling of dependence.[53]

In such a position, the individual invariably becomes lost or absorbed within God, or God becomes nothing but an expression of the individual. Here, it seems that something of the former took place. Redemption by Christ became identified with influence, in Schleiermacher's thought.[54] In his system, Jesus became the context of forgiveness. Personal expression, as the instrument, was absorbed into that context. This was a form of reductionism that made Jesus almost irrelevant when it came to realizing forgiveness. Jesus as an influence may be a part of the mediation of the context of forgiveness. Yet, influence is not *the* context any more than, in Chapter 2, acceptance was *the* context. This complete altering of the original ideas of redemption is made clear when Schleiermacher said, " The term ' redemption ' is not suitable for this new communication of a powerful God-consciousness." With that statement, Schleiermacher bypassed completely the need and place for instrumentation. He had brought his whole theology within the contextual dimension of forgiveness, and, by so doing, had lost the relevancy he so clearly desired.

The great work of Albrecht Ritschl is *The Christian Doctrine of Justification and Reconciliation*. The title itself suggests his concern for the question of forgiveness. Ritschl tried to begin where Schleiermacher ended in making the faith relevant. He sought to make a positive theological attack on the basis of a true awareness of the Reformers. His studies convinced him that the immediate object of theological knowledge is the community's faith that it stands to God in a relation that is essentially established and determined by forgiveness. To this end, he began his book by saying:

Now it is not sufficient for my purpose to bring out what Jesus has said about the forgiveness of sins attached to His person and His death. For even if His statements might seem perfectly clear, their significance becomes intelligible only when we see how they are reflected in the consciousness of those who believe in Him, and how the members of the Christian community trace back their consciousness of pardon to the Person and the action and passion of Jesus.[55]

Ritschl made the notable contribution of bringing forgiveness back to the center of the arena in theological thinking. He was aware of the danger of seeing forgiveness in just a pietistic context; he spoke of the need for forgiveness to be an actual experience. We must not deny the " principle of the Reformation that justification as actual fact becomes a matter of experience through discharge of moral tasks, while these are to be discharged in the labours of one's vocations." [56] This thinking is in line with my view that forgiveness must be experienced as a context and expressed as an instrument by the forgiving of others.

However, in the light of the typology of forgiveness that evolved in my parish experience, Ritschl made fundamentally the same mistake as Schleiermacher. Karl Barth and Paul Lehmann are clearly right in observing that forgiveness again became a matter of human action alone. Ritschl erred in identifying his theology with the realization of forgiveness instead of seeing that the experience of forgiveness was but the door through which to pass for one's theology.

In addition, Ritschl erred in identifying the forgiveness of sins and justification. This error is an outgrowth of his failure to see the difference between systematic theology and pastoral theology. He wrote:

The ground of justification, or the forgiveness of sins [note the identification] is the benevolent, gracious, merciful purpose of God to vouchsafe to sinful men the privilege of access to Himself. The form in which sinners appropriate this gift is faith, that is, emotional trust in God, accompanied by the conviction of the value of this gift for one's blessedness which, called forth by God's grace, takes the place of the former mistrust which was bound up with the feeling of guilt.[57]

This meant that, for Ritschl too, the forgiveness of sins was identified with the *context* of forgiveness. The result was that redemption, in and of itself, was reduced to a matter of emotion. For Ritschl said: " Christ comes to act upon the individual believer on the one hand through the historical remembrance of Him which is possible in the Church, on the other hand as the permanent Author of all the influences and impulses " that come from men.[58] " Influence " and " redemption " had again been equated, and influence had come to be identified with context. Once again, the awareness of the need for the context of forgiveness had resulted in the loss of the instrumentation of it and the reduction of forgiveness to an understandable but irrelevant human feeling.

When the church becomes just human, it has no more to say than any of the human sciences of man. As a church, it has become irrelevant to the crises of life. When the crisis comes, and a minister faces his congregation, he needs a rediscovery of the faith. Hence, when war came in the twentieth century, Barth faced his congregation, and the world needed *Der Römerbrief*, his rediscovery of faith.

VI THE AMERICAN SCENE

This chapter cannot close without a word about what has been happening on the American scene. Mention has been made of Jonathan Edwards. After him, in the nineteenth century, America began the change from a frontier to a rural and from a rural to an industrial nation. To the problems of that kind of world, the Christian faith seemed irrelevant. The highly rigid and systematic statements of the faith were dominant. Into this picture came Walter Rauschenbusch.

Rauschenbusch, who died in 1918, came from a background of German pietism. Hence, it can be assumed that he was acquainted with the contextual dimension of forgiveness. However, the forgiveness he had seen and heard was always expressed in individualistic terms. Regardless of what one may or may not think of his theology, it is to the everlasting credit of Rauschenbusch that he brought to the fore the full dimension of sin. He recognized that awareness of one's individual sin can be merely an escape from doing anything about the social expression of that sin. He recognized that the identification of sin with sex or murder could be a means of blinding oneself to the depth of sin. His fundamental insight is expressed in the opening of one of his major books as follows:

For the last ten years, our nation has been under conviction of sin. We had long been living a double life, but without realizing it. Our business methods and the principles of our religion and of our democracy have always been at strife, but not until our sin had matured and brought forth wholesale death did we understand our own obliquity.[59]

Rauschenbusch made it clear that sin had a social dimension and that the answer to sin had a social dimension. The gospel was not only personal but also social.

In expressing the theology of this gospel, he considered the concept of the Kingdom of God as central. All theology should develop from that point.[60] In this view, Rauschenbusch was expressing the need for the context of forgiveness. As in other expressions with regard to this context, he too held that freedom was in relation to the context. "We walk by faith. Every human life is so placed that it can share with God in the creation of the Kingdom, or can resist and retard its progress."[61] Man was free to do either.

Insofar as Rauschenbusch broadened the concept of sin so that its social dimension is clear, and insofar as he broadened the concept of forgiveness or redemption so that their social dimensions are clear, his work stands as a contribution to the realization of forgiveness. Forgiveness cannot be realized if it does not take into account the social as well as the individual aspects.

Whether or not one agrees with his doctrine of Christ or his view of Scripture, however, Rauschenbusch made the same error in America that Schleiermacher and Ritschl made in Europe. He had identified the instrumentation of forgiveness with its context. He came to identify the Kingdom of God with "social justice, prosperity, and happiness."[62] "The Kingdom of God is humanity organized according to the will of God." [63] It is true that love of neighbor cannot be separated from love of God. Again, however, neither can they be made identical. What has been shown about the realization of forgiveness allows for only one reply to his position. "Social justice, prosperity, happiness and humanity organized" are the instrumentations of the Kingdom of God. They are not *the* Kingdom of God. It is not, as he believed, that "a change in penology may be an evidence of salvation," [64] but that a change in penology may be the instrumentation by which a society makes salvation real. In the sense in which he combined them, Rauschenbusch has done with sociology what Schleiermacher and Ritschl did with psychology. He has drawn too close an identification between human emotion and the totality of Christian truth.

Further, Rauschenbusch has used the matter of instrumentation in an almost Lutheran sense — when he has used it. He criticized the parish because "it lacks an ethical imperative which can induce repentance." [65] Rauschenbusch would seek a law or an ethic that would make men wish to repent; but again I ask, "How can they understand that ethic apart from the context of forgiveness?" Thus, he who pioneered in making the faith relevant to society as Schleiermacher and Ritschl pioneered in making the faith relevant to the individual person removed that which would make forgiveness real. He reminded us of the context, and himself lost the place of the instrument.

If in Europe the stage was set for *Der Römerbrief*, in America, it was ready for *The Nature and Destiny of Man*.

6

"Realized Forgiveness" in the Body of Christ—Alone

I THE DYNAMICS OF "REALIZED FORGIVENESS": CONCLUSIONS

WHEN a pastor faces a parishioner, when a congregation faces itself, or when a church faces the world, what is the question that each hears asked? For every person in every age, the basic question will be asked in a different way. For one it will be, "What must I do to be saved?" For the rich young ruler it was, "What lack I yet?" For Viktor Frankl, in the death camps of Nazi Germany, it was the search for meaning. No matter how it is asked, however, it is basically the same question: "How can I be whole?"

It may be dangerous to generalize about the whole United States from a few congregations. Yet, on the basis of what I have heard in the congregations I have served, in the synagogues I have visited, in suburbia and out of suburbia, the real question being asked by the twentieth-century American living under the threat of the bomb is this: "How do I maintain my integrity — now?" For the person in the early church or at the time of Luther, the concern may well have been for oneness with God after death — i.e., tomorrow. This is not true today. Mrs. A, whose case was discussed in Chapter 1, said: "I am so involved in sending children to school, doing dishes, and preparing meals for my husband, I don't have time to think of tomorrow. All I know is that something is wrong today, and I want an answer for today." The twentieth-century American does not need to be told that the evils of the day are sufficient thereof; he knows it. He may be determined to find an escape just for today. He does not hear the argument that sex, drugs, or liquor will bring consequences for

tomorrow. He is concerned about *today*. Nor is this concern altogether bad; for whatever the problem, twentieth-century men and
women are determined to find a solution now. The modern American does not hear the warning that a courageous stand today may
cost one's life tomorrow (witness Mr. Evers of the South). He
must meet the present.

Students of personality may note that concentration on the day
is characteristic of a child. " Lack of concern for tomorrow indicates lack of maturity," they say. So be it. We are all children —
beginners — in the art of living in an atomic age. Anxiety leads
to infantile reactions, and we are in an age of anxiety. " How
can I maintain my integrity now? " is still the question. It is a
desire for wholeness in the face of fragmentation. It is a desire
for personality in the face of automation. It is an East Orange
housewife in a family discussion group asking: " What do I do
to find myself? I have had a college education, but I am hemmed
in by diapers. And I feel guilty, because radio commentators say
I should get out more; but I can't." [1]

The thesis of these pages is that the answer begins with " realized forgiveness." It is forgiveness as a reality in one's life that
makes one free to be oneself. It is forgiveness as a reality in one's
life that brings to personal awareness those things which make
for wholeness — those things which make for peace.

In all that has gone before, " realized forgiveness " has been defined as an experience and not as a word. Just as the basic questions of life are always the same, but the words for expressing
those questions change, so with forgiveness: the words that describe " realized forgiveness " change, but not the experience.
This experience has been identified in the preceding pages as that
which gives one the freedom to be creative because it allows one
to be a new creator. Today, large masses of people throughout the
world do not use the words " sin " and " forgiveness "; but they
do seek this basic event in their lives. Where will they find it?
Only in Jesus Christ or in that which is truly the church (the
body of Christ). Why? Because Jesus Christ represents both the
mediation and the instrumentation of forgiveness in relation to
all of life. Consider the following:

One pole of the experience of forgiveness is the pole of context.

Forgiveness is a context in which we live. I have said that this context is mediated by a person or a group. This context leaves a person or a group free to do two things. First, it gives freedom for honest introspection. As Robert Burns expressed it: " O wad some Pow'r the giftie gie us, To see oursels as others see us! " The context gives the individual the freedom to see himself as he is. The context also gives the group the freedom to see itself as it is. Second, the context gives the freedom to see that one is not bound to what one is. One of the most revealing modern demonstrations of this has been by the Negroes in the civil rights movement. From my talks with various ones involved in sit-ins, beatings, and violence, a difference among them has become clear to me. There are those who are not acting but simply reacting. They resent the situation in which they find themselves and lash out at it. Others, as expressed repeatedly in the writings of Martin Luther King, are aware not only of the nature of their bondage and its hold upon the soul of the Negro but of the nature of what they can be. The mood is not one of revenge for past wrongs, but, as expressed in Paul, one of pressing on " toward the goal for the prize of the upward call of God in Christ Jesus."

It is the Christian faith that there is not only a context of forgiveness, but also a mediation of this context. The mediation is Jesus Christ. In order to be whole, it is to the mediation of this context that the person and the group must be obedient. This is a matter of faith. If Christ is not this mediator, full freedom is not possible.

The other pole of the experience is the pole of instrumentation. I have said that " instrumentation " is that which gives adequate expression to the context as mediated. This refers to those moments when one hears a speech and then says, " I always knew it, but I never could put it into words." Until one could " put it into words," the " it " was never really known. The words were the very instrument by which " it " became real. Thus, the instrumentation of forgiveness is that which allows forgiveness to become fully real.

As with the pole of context, the instrumentation does two things for the person or the group. First, the instrument is that which expresses things as they are, that is, it is a genuine confession of sin. Second, it is that which expresses things as they have become. In the pole of context, freedom is there, but not expressed. In the pole of instrumentation, freedom is expressed. Whereas seeing things as they are is a genuine confession of sin, seeing things as they have become is a genuine confession of faith.

To be grasped properly, " realized forgiveness " must be understood in both social and individual terms. This is why care has been taken in the preceding paragraphs to speak of the individual *and* the group — that is, both Christ and the church are necessary.

This point is clearly seen in the Scriptures in the concept of the covenant coupled with a view of the suffering servant. It has not always been seen in the history of Christian thought. It was part of the genius of the Reformation to expound the corporate dimension of life in its relation to the Christian faith. Since then, however, pietism has tended to emphasize the individual, and the social gospel has tended to emphasize the group. In the concept of " realized forgiveness," this separation cannot be tolerated because man himself is not so separated.

On an individual basis, the mediation is expressed through Christ as a person. Thus, at the foot of the cross, the centurion is compelled to say, " Truly this was the Son of God! " In relation to other people, however, this mediation is expressed through the church which is called " the body of Christ." Precisely where we find this " body of Christ " or this church is another question. It may be that it cannot be found in any religious group! Wherever it is found, however, it must mediate the forgiving presence of God.

A similar point can be made with regard to the instrumentation of forgiveness. As instruments, the cross and the empty tomb express the context of the oneness with God. Therefore, the Scripture speaks of God being in Christ and reconciling the world to him. Paul, speaking of our sufferings, points to what happened to Christ and says: " I am sure that neither . . . height, nor depth, nor anything else in all creation, will be able to separate us from the love of God in Christ Jesus our Lord " (Rom. 8:38-39). Jesus Christ, as a person, is the instrument of the forgiveness of God.

The Christian fellowship is the instrument that makes real the context of forgiveness. The form of this instrumentation is always some form of service. Jesus washed the feet of the disciples. He said, " As you did it to one of the least of these my brethren, you did it to me." This service is not only a service of helping others; it is also a service of fellowship with others and of forgiving others. Nothing expresses fellowship and forgiveness as much as does breaking bread together.[2] Thus Jesus said: " For as often as you eat this bread and drink the cup, you proclaim the Lord's death until he comes." The act of communing together is the act that can symbolize the forgiveness we have of one another. Thereby it makes real the context that Christ mediated in his death and that leads us to know " this is the Son of God."

It is at this point that the church as a parish has its importance. Whether in the pulpit, around the Lord's Table, in the choir stall, in the pew, or on the street, the church is not important because of the good influence it has on the community. It is not important because of the charity that we can render through it. The parish is important because we need it in order to make real God's forgiveness of ourselves. Paul was not a missionary because he was a Christian. Paul became one with God through the instrumentation of being a missionary. He had to be a missionary. A man becomes a part of the church, not because he is a Christian, but because the church is the instrumentation by which he makes real his relationship with Christ.

I always rebel at the answer that my confirmation classes invariably give when I ask, " Why do you want to unite with the church? " " To know more about Christ," they say. I rebel because I have always understood this to mean a search for intellectual knowledge. Now, studying the dynamics of forgiveness, I am convinced that, in a different sense, the instinct of these teenagers is right. Until they can find that which gives adequate expression to their relationship with God, they do not know Christ.

Why should they seek this expression through the church? Why not through Alcoholics Anonymous? Why not through the psychotherapist who operates completely outside the context of the church, yet still mediates a context of love and concern?

The first question is answered by remembering that the church must never be confused with the institution. The institution of the fellowship or the denomination may indeed fail to be the church. The context may indeed crop up elsewhere. When the church as an institution fails, I am sure that the context is expressed elsewhere. However, I do insist upon the importance of the parish in some visible form. At its best, the institution is an extension of the parish. The fact that the parish often seems dominated by institutional concerns does not remove the necessity for the parish. For the context to be mediated and the instrumentation to be adequate, there must be a visible expression that relates to the historical and to the present body of Christ. It is this truth upon which the Roman Catholic and Orthodox churches are insisting when they call for the continuity of the church. Disagreement as to what that " continuity " means must not result in forgetting the necessity and reality of a continuity.

There is another answer to the question about groups outside the parish, such as Alcoholics Anonymous. Good as they are, they never will be what they could be apart from a genuine expression of the visible context and instrumentation of forgiveness. Jesus spoke of none on earth being greater than John the Baptist. Yet he who was least in the Kingdom of Heaven was greater than the Baptist. In the same sense, a therapist may be tremendously helpful; but the person being helped will never achieve what he could achieve in answer to his quest for wholeness, apart from some visible expression of God's forgiveness. I define a parish as the place where this expression takes place.

Today, it is popular to criticize the parish. Today, many would " give up " on the parish. To these, I reply that the parish is important not because it succeeds or fails, but because it is the one fellowship that is concerned about the totality of " realized forgiveness."

Service organizations and labor unions are instrument-conscious. They are concerned with works of service. They do good work, but they are so involved in the instrumentations of life that they completely neglect the context. Cell groups tend to be just instrument-conscious or context-conscious — depending upon their particular state of development. Whether the group is Alcoholics Anonymous, an ethical culture group, or some form of cell group, each runs the typical history of a sect. When it begins, it is a revolt in some form from the identification of wholeness with the expression of wholeness. It begins as a group trying to mediate the context of concern. However, it is now commonplace knowledge that a sect quickly becomes a denomination. Concern for the organization means concern for the instrument as opposed to the context. This shift always happens when the desire for the instrumentation that makes the context real becomes so great that the initial purpose is lost. The church is essential because it is the one fellowship of people that is consciously concerned with keeping *both* poles of " realized forgiveness." It is the parish where this concern is most clearly manifested.

The parish quest for " realized forgiveness " can be seen in many ways throughout history. It can be seen in the history of church architecture. From the cathedrals with their great altars to the Friends' meetinghouses without even a table, the architecture reflects the way people have understood forgiveness and sought to experience it. Perhaps the parish quest can most clearly be observed in the liturgy of worship. Each change can be seen as an effort to make forgiveness real in the parish. A study of the trends in worship in Bard Thompson's *Liturgies of the Western Church* [3] shows a simple and straightforward liturgy in the early church. In the mid-second century, added to the Sacrament was a kiss. " Our prayers being ended, we greet one another with a kiss," said the Apology of Justin Martyr.[4]

As the years went on, more and more was added to the simple rite. In the Middle Ages, three areas of the Mass were clearly distinguishable. Thompson describes them as:

(1) The Mass as an " epiphany " of God amongst men, which focuses attention upon the reality of the Eucharistic Presence, upon the Consecration at which it occurred, and upon the priest by whose action it was effected; (2) the Mass as a sacrifice offered unto God for the benefit of the living and the dead; and (3) the Mass as an allegorical drama of the whole economy of redemption.[5]

Although Protestants would react against points within these three sections, such as " the Mass as a sacrifice," the importance of the three sections should not be missed. The first centers upon the context of the forgiveness of God. The service begins by calling attention to the reality of a mediator that is present. The second section is the negative dimension of confession. That is, the sacrifice is for that which has been done that should not have been done. Out of the freedom to see what was wrong, one is then free to see what one has become in Christ. Therefore, the third section of the Mass centered on the positive affirmation of faith.

Thus, the liturgy of the first fifteen centuries represented the desire and the effort on the part of the parish to mediate and make real the forgiveness of God. The same is true of the Reformation. In the parish, and out of a feeling that forgiveness was not being realized, Luther placed his ninety-five theses. The Reformation, particularly in Switzerland, rethought and reconstituted an entirely new liturgy. In 1524, Bucer gave a radical reshaping of the liturgy by saying that, when the congregation comes together, the minister is to admonish them to confess and to pray for pardon. The contextual dimension is expressed when the minister, in the words of Bucer, "confesses to God on behalf of the whole congregation, prays for pardon, and proclaims the remission of sins to those that believe." [6] Note, in connection with the earlier discussion about Luther, that it is *after* the confession that the congregation "sings again the Ten Commandments or something else." [7] It is from that point that the service moves to the gospel and the confession of faith.

In our own day, the renewed interest in liturgy, and the tone of the studies by Howard Hageman and Donald MacLeod reflect the concern of the parish to make forgiveness real. In the Roman Catholic Church, parts continued to be added to the Mass until it became unbearable. Is it just coincidence that a "pastor" pope called the Second Vatican Council and set as one of the central tasks of that Council the revising of the liturgy?

The dynamic of "realized forgiveness" must be a central concern of the church. Without it, the church is nothing more than an institution with a religion and a form. With it, the church is a fellowship with a faith it has learned to express. To find this dynamic is the central concern of the parish.

II THE SIGNIFICANCE OF "REALIZED FORGIVENESS" FOR THEOLOGY

Ever since the Reformation, the church in the West has tried to develop a theology that could come to terms with the Renaissance, the Enlightenment, and the development of science in both its Newtonian and Einsteinian phases. In Roman Catholicism, this was done by building on the thought of Saint Thomas which placed all areas of knowledge in a manageable structure. The weakness in that structure was the ease with which it led to seeing life in watertight compartments instead of seeing it as a whole. Further, to Protestant eyes, this structure came to be concentrated too much on the instrumentation of forgiveness and not on the context.

In Protestantism, there were attempts to succeed where Saint Thomas had failed. One such attempt was called " Biblical literalism." Literalism tried to meet the Enlightenment by paying no attention to it. In reaction to that effort came liberalism as seen in Schleiermacher. Liberalism tried to meet the developing sciences by taking scientific thought patterns and clearly demarcating the area of religion in relation to human experience. As liberalism reacted to literalism, neoorthodoxy responded to liberalism. Neoorthodoxy was a return to the revelation of God as the sole basis of judgment, but with awareness that literalism was never a guarantee of the Word of God. Although existentialism had been evident for much of this time, it was not until after World War II that it gained the public attention and impact that neoorthodoxy had had. There may be a question as to whether or not it ever reached the acclaim of neoorthodoxy. Nevertheless, fifteen years after the close of World War II, Paul Tillich universally (not just in liberal schools) shares as much of the spotlight as the neoorthodox.

The most recent attempt to meet the developments of science is pastoral theology. It has by no means reached the stature of any of the other schools of thought, and perhaps it never will. Regardless, pastoral theology is misunderstood today if it is thought of as an attempt to describe the mechanics of church life. On the contrary, pastoral theology is properly understood only when seen as another approach to a unified body of theological knowledge that stands in legitimate relation to other bodies of knowledge such as philosophy and physics.

The significance of pastoral theology, therefore, is to be understood as theology in a new key. As such, pastoral theology is just beginning to find itself. The man who has been most articulate in this awareness of pastoral theology as a theology is Seward Hiltner. Surely he is the first to have attempted a self-conscious statement of such a theology. However, the Episcopalian, Reuel Howe, the Methodists, Carroll Wise and Paul Johnson, the Baptist, Wayne Oates, and the European pastor, Eduard Thurneysen, are a few of a larger number who should be mentioned in the same breath.

As was indicated in the opening chapter, pastoral theology says that all theologies, since the end of the first century, have made a basic error. They have not recognized the place of pastoral theology in the totality of the theological conversation. This means that they have not recognized the significance of " realized forgiveness " as the starting place for any theological discussion. Whether or not the new movement in pastoral theology will meet the need remains to be seen. In the past, pastoral theology has failed because it has itself not recognized its position in relation to the total theological enterprise. Now that that error is being overcome, history will have to judge whether or not pastoral theology has succeeded in being true to both sides of " realized forgiveness " and whether or not it has become absorbed, like the others, in one of the two polarities. History now moves at such a rate that the answer may not be long in coming.   .

This new key says that theology has to be written in the context of freedom. There is a sense in which theology is itself a part of the instrumentation of that freedom. Theology is a part of the confession of faith in which forgiveness becomes real. Therefore it is not enough to say that pastoral theology is the preface to all theology. It also must be added that theology-in-general completes pastoral theology and speaks back to it. The very fact that forgiveness as a realized experience is dynamic and not static and the fact that life is always changing and always needing new expression make this so.

This point is not strange to the Eastern Orthodox Church which has a deep awareness of its theology being expressed in its liturgy, and its liturgy, in a real sense, being its theology. Neither is the point strange to Karl Barth, who made the shift from Christian dogmatics to church dogmatics. The point is strange,

though, to the American mind and to all who are influenced by
the American mind; for the American has learned to live com-
partmentally. He lives in one place, works in another, and plays
in yet another. The idea is strange to all theologies in that no
current system, including Barth's, has adequately considered the
beginning point of the freedom that is made real in forgiveness.

It would be too long a process to look at every major theologian
in relation to the concept of " realized forgiveness." The task
would be almost endless if one or more of these theologies were
to be analyzed in detail from this perspective. However, a few
representative theologians can be seen to demonstrate that the
initial point of " realized forgiveness " has been missed. There is
more to be said than the references on method in Chapter 2.

If there is any one theologian who seems to come close to the
point of view of pastoral theology it is Karl Barth. He has taken
the church seriously — and by " church " is meant the fellowship
or community of believers. Perhaps more than any other theologian, Barth has kept close to the experience of the worshiping
community in his own activity as a pastor in prison work.

In one of his early books, *God in Action*, Barth suggests that
everything depends upon what God has done in Christ. By this,
Barth starts, not with God as the creator, but with God as the
" new creator " in Christ. This is another way of speaking of the
context of forgiveness. The whole ministry, then, is an instrumentation of that context; for " the ministry of the Word of God
is primarily and decidedly a service of which we ourselves have
need, and which the Word of God itself shows us, and will continue to show unto us." [8] This is precisely the point of pastoral
theology.

To show that this viewpoint has not been lost over a span of
thirty years, one need look no farther than the book that con-
tains his retirement lectures and the lectures given on his tour of
America. Barth writes: " Before human thought and speech can
respond to God's word, they have to be summoned into existence
and given reality by the creative act of God's word. Without the
precedence of the creative Word, there can be not only no proper
theology but, in fact, no evangelical theology at all! " [9] Again, he
says, " It is clear that evangelical theology itself can only be pneu-

matic, spiritual theology." [10] Thus, in the first five chapters of the book, Barth describes the place of context. The remaining twelve chapters (lectures) are really the instrumentation of that theology. He gives means by which the context is expressed in the instrumentation of wonder, concern, commitment, faith, solitude, doubt, temptation, hope, prayer, study, service, and love.

What, then, is the objection to Barth's position? From the standpoint of pastoral theology, there are three objections. To make the point, consider the following quotations. After speaking of the way theology sometimes resists submission to the Spirit, Barth says:

As soon as the Spirit begins to stir within it [theology], it suspects the danger of fanaticism; or it may rotate in circles of historicism, rationalism, moralism, romanticism, dogmaticism, or intellectualism.[11]

There is no time or situation in which theology can allow itself to recognize some general regulation as a binding law for its viewpoints, conceptions, images, and speech. And by no means may theology let itself be bound by any such regulation that rules or desires to rule at the present. It makes no difference whether this regulation is proclaimed in the name of Aristotle, Descartes, Kant, Hegel, or Heidegger.[12]

Barth is here ruling out questions from the human situation that come from outside the church. This position is sound for the same reason that Luther's use of law was considered unsound. It is only within the context of the church that the human situation can be understood. The first criticism of Barth's position, however, is that he does not make room for the " regulations " and questions about the human situation when asked from *within* the church. From Barth's point of view, the psychiatrist in describing the human situation can do no more than write a footnote to what is already revealed about the estrangement of man from God. From the point of view of pastoral theology, however, what does it mean to say that " the word of God is not fettered " (II Tim. 2:9) and that " the Wind blows where it wills; . . . so it is with every one who is born of the Spirit " (John 3:8) ? I understand these texts to mean that *within* the context of God's forgiveness, the human situation can say something concrete about the nature of sin expressed and the nature of faith experienced within a given moment of time.

Further, it is the very freedom that comes from forgiveness that makes it possible not to be bound to the "regulation that rules" in the culture of an Aristotle, Descartes, Kant, Hegel, or Heidegger. By trying to protect theology from the presuppositions of a non-Christian experience, and by overreacting to the psychologizing of Ritschl, Barth has removed the very thing that can free theology from bondage to philosophy or existence. It is not ignoring philosophical or psychological thought that makes theology pure. It is the realization of forgiveness that accomplishes the goal.

The second criticism of Barth's position is that he has tended to identify theology with what is here called the instrumentation of forgiveness.

In his theological writing, he points to the necessity of everything's depending on the grace of God — i.e., on the context of forgiveness. The theological enterprise itself, however, he identifies entirely with what I call the instrument of forgiveness. He does that when he says that every minister has to be a theologian — always. In Barth's thought, only by standing in the context of God's grace and using the instrument of theological thought can the ministry be a Christian ministry.

Here, Karl Barth is subject to the same criticism as Augustine. By identifying the context of Christian experience with grace, the place and function of instrument becomes warped. Although there is a sense in which theology is part of what makes forgiveness real, theology and the instrumentation of forgiveness are not identical. Initially, *everyone* must feel the freedom from bondage that forgiveness gives before he can move into "logic-centered" theology. Forgiveness must be realized. Before theological thinking can take place, both dimensions of forgiveness must be in effect. When that happens, true theological conversation is possible. To the degree that it does not happen, one does not act in conversation; one only reacts in talk.[13]

The third criticism of Barth's position is that it leads to a subtle mixing of the two parts of the experience of forgiveness. This is seen, for example, when Eduard Thurneysen says that the totality of man is a "datum which is not to be explained by psychological methodologies but only to be described phenomenologically."[14]

The fact that there is a part that cannot be described does not mean that what can be described is not a part of the experience of forgiveness. The " phenomenological part " is the instrumentation that brings into awareness what cannot otherwise be touched. The confusing of the two areas and the treating of the two as though they were one is, in fact, the same fundamental error that was made by Schleiermacher and Ritschl. It is the insight of pastoral theology that both areas must be held in tension.

The outgrowth of this error is that Barth and Schleiermacher both ascribe pastoral theology to the same place. Wrote the former: " So-called ' practical theology ' . . . has been unjustly treated as a stepchild of theological science. It has been entrusted to those persons who were considered insignificant or just good enough for the position. Schleiermacher was right when he called practical theology the ' crown of theology.' " [15] Pastoral theology has importance; but in their view, it is the fruit of theology. The crown is that with which the main body is " topped off " — to take a phrase from construction work.

In the writings of Paul Tillich, one sees the opposite of the position in neoorthodoxy. Whereas neoorthodoxy, and Barth in particular, paid attention to the position of the church in the possibility of theology and ruled out the place of human datum, Tillich sees the place of human datum and pays insufficient heed to the place of the church.

Tillich is correct not only in seeing the importance of pastoral theology, but also in rejecting the " crown " analogy:

The organization of theological work is not complete without the inclusion of what is usually called " practical theology." Although Schleiermacher praised it as the crown of theology, it is not a third part in addition to the historical and the systematic parts. It is the technical theory through which these two parts are applied to the life of the church. A technical theory describes the adequate means for a given end.[16]

However, this point of view sees pastoral theology as a bridge between the world of the church and the world of culture.[17] As such, pastoral theology really does not become a part of the theological dialogue at all. Its function becomes one of interpreting the dialogue to the church or the world, or conveying the questions from the world to the dialogue; but in and of itself it never becomes the vestibule through which one must pass to engage in dialogue.

The reason for this position is Tillich's view of theological method. Briefly, his view is that, in the method of correlation, theology gives the Christian answer to the human question. For him, systematic theology, " makes an analysis of the human situation out of which the existential questions arise, and it demonstrates that the symbols used in the Christian message are the answers to those questions." [18]

Perhaps no theologian has done more than Paul Tillich to illuminate the relevance of existential insight and analysis for the Christian faith. However, his view of correlation ultimately suffers from the same weakness as Luther's view of law. As the law made clear the sin to which the gospel must speak, Tillich's existential question makes clear the relevant problem to which the theologian must speak. From the perspective of pastoral theology, this statement is challenged on the basis that only *within* the context of forgiveness can the existential question really be asked.

Tillich's position leads him to say that the courage of a man " to be " is great courage. It brings man face to face with the ground of all being — i.e., with God. " One could say," he writes, " that the courage to be is the courage to accept oneself as accepted in spite of being unacceptable." [19] He equates acceptance with the doctrines of justification by faith and forgiveness of sins. " The courage to be . . . is the courage to accept the forgiveness of sins, not as an abstract assertion but as the fundamental experience in the encounter with God." [20]

In view of what has previously been said about the difference between acceptance and forgiveness, and in view of the error of putting the existential question outside the context of forgiveness, this position of Tillich's must be reversed. By his statement he takes account of suffering in forgiveness. However, rather than seeing the " courage to be " first, and forgiveness as involved in it, the order should be reversed. The forgiveness of sins should be seen first, and the " courage to be," subsumed within it. It is " realized forgiveness " that makes one free to have the courage to be. On the surface, the difference may be slight. Yet the differences at the bottom may be as great as East and West.

In bringing to a close these words on the relation between pastoral theology and theology-in-general, mention should be made both of Nicolas Berdyaev and Reinhold Niebuhr. The former brings us again in touch with the climate of Eastern Orthodoxy. The latter brings us to the present day in America — even though it is hard to "type" him.

Berdyaev has been called the "apostle of freedom." [21] His thought is stimulating and helpful. Further, it too does not easily allow itself to be labeled. As he said, although he reflected the Eastern and Orthodox worlds, his thought is his own.[22] In the last few pages of his comprehensive book, *The Beginning and the End,* he shows a position of grace and freedom that is much like the position of pastoral theology and the position of the Eastern side of the early church. Yet, what is here called instrumentation he tended to rule out as the "objectifying" of that which is not an object.[23] Further, he began his work on the premise of man's search for freedom and meaning. Helpful as his thinking is, it is a further demonstration of what happens when the full concept of the realization of forgiveness is not taken seriously. One side of the concept is dealt with to the detriment, if not the exclusion of the other.

Reinhold Niebuhr is equally difficult to type. He has been called neoorthodox, but he so clearly bears the stamp of American practicality that his neoorthodoxy and that of Barth often seem quite removed. It is also difficult to analyze his position because he did not develop a system, as did Barth and Brunner, but rather sought to develop an ethic for an age of industrial might, population explosion, and high-rise apartments. His concern to relate the structures of power and the context of living makes his thought in many ways analogous to that which has been said here in the name of pastoral theology.

However, the sense in which Niebuhr is neoorthodox and like Barth is the point at which the position of pastoral theology raises its question. As with Barth, Niebuhr does not allow for the legitimate dimension of the instrumentation of forgiveness. He writes:

The Christian answer to the human predicament, a divine mercy toward man, revealed in Christ, which is at once a power enabling the self to realize itself truly beyond itself in love, and the forgiveness of God toward the self . . . is an answer which grows out of and which in turn helps to create the radical Christian concept of human freedom. In the Christian faith the self in its final freedom does not find its norm in the structures either of nature or of reason.[24]

Again as with Barth, the warning against identifying forgiveness with the structures of life is right. Yet Niebuhr does not give structure the legitimate place it must have as the instrumentation of forgiveness. That place becomes clear only in a total view of " realized forgiveness."

When taken seriously, the theological contribution of " realized forgiveness " is the contribution of making it possible to achieve that of which Barth, Niebuhr, Berdyaev, and Tillich speak. " Realized forgiveness " gives a basis for a common theological language because it relates the meaning of words to the actual experience discussed. " Realized forgiveness " also gives a basis for understanding the problem of meeting the secularist and of interpreting why we do not break through to him. Finally, " realized forgiveness " gives a basis for the witness of the church to the world. It suggests that the only witness is to say to the man of the world: " Come and see for yourself. In the context of forgiveness, have the courage to be forgiven, and know the truth that makes you free."

It is because I see " realized forgiveness " as the area on which pastoral theology centers, that I see pastoral theology not as the crown of theology but as the footstool, not as the chancel but as the outer vestibule.

III   THE SIGNIFICANCE FOR PASTORAL THEOLOGY

The question now arises as to whether or not it is legitimate to identify " realized forgiveness " with pastoral theology. In the introduction to his book, Seward Hiltner points out that since the days of the Reformation, the term " pastoral " has been used in two ways. It has been used to describe the work of the pastor so that everything the pastor did was, by definition, pastoral. It was also used to define the particular function of caring for the flock.[25]

Hiltner noted truth and danger in both views. The first approach was right in that there indeed is a pastoral dimension to everything a minister does. The second approach was right because there are certain activities of a minister that are predominantly pastoral. By the same measure, this second approach taken alone is inadequate because it confines " pastoral " too narrowly. Taken alone, the first suggestion is wrong because it leads to an imperialistic approach — as though there is nothing else to pastoral work.

In order to solve the problem, Hiltner suggests that what is distinctive about pastoral theology lies, not in the offices or functions of the minister, but in the *perspective*. As I have noted, he suggests that there is one body of theological knowledge that is " logic-centered." This includes systematic theology, Biblical theology, and their counterparts. On the other side, there is that body of theological knowledge which is " operational." One area of this is the shepherding area. The other two areas that he identifies are the organizing and the communicating areas.[26] Each of these other areas is set apart because each has a particular perspective.

There is a temptation to equate preaching with the communicative, administration with the organizing, and counseling with the shepherding perspectives. To do so is to miss Hiltner's insight and important contribution. For there is a matter of administration involved in counseling just as there is a place for counseling or pastoral care in the way one handles one's administration. Again, it is the perspective of an area that makes the difference; it is not the particular activity of that office.

It is not possible to correlate Hiltner's constructive statement and mine. In following the lead of the Reformation, he has identified " pastoral theology " in relation to the minister. Whether it is spoken of as pastoral care or as everything the minister does, the focus is still on the minister. By contrast, I have identified pastoral theology, not with the minister, but with the ministry of the congregation. I have wanted to find that perspective which gives a unity to all aspects of the church's ministry, and which relates the ministry integrally with the " logic-centered " disciplines.

In considering this perspective, there is a danger in giving too much attention to the Reformation. John T. McNeill stated that the Reformation had its inception in those affairs which concerned the cure of souls. However, on the basis of McNeill's study, the danger of the Reformation was overreaction to the flagrant abuses within the church. As church history was traced back to the early days, two points emerged (Chapter 4). One was that the perspective which was central to the matter of the cure of souls was the perspective of forgiveness made real. The second was that this was an exercise of the total church.

In view of this, the approach of this book has been to define pastoral theology in relation to the experience of "realized forgiveness." The moment that is done, pastoral theology cannot be limited to counseling, preaching, or any other area. To do so would be to place any of those areas in a tyrannical position with regard to the other areas. The imperative for seeing the perspective of "realized forgiveness" is twofold. Initially, it puts the whole concept of the ministry into focus. It does not prejudge the nature of any area or office, but speaks to all areas and offices within the church. It also *requires* a place for laymen as well as clergy. Shepherding, as an attitude, is a requirement for both. "Realized forgiveness," as a perspective of the ministry of the parish, demands the total community. It requires the total community of believers to mediate the context of forgiveness and it requires the total community of believers to give the instrumentation of that context. In this, the ministry of the pastor is a part, but *only* a part of the total ministry.

In the picture that I have presented, then, pastoral theology has a specific definition: pastoral theology is the theology of church ministry that finds its center in the perspective of " realized forgiveness " and that thereby forms the foundation for the theological enterprise of which it is a part.

In the history of the church, there seem to have been four areas of concern that relate, in emphasis, to the two poles identified in the realization of forgiveness. These are the areas of communication, nurture, discipline, and shepherding. At the heart of communication is confrontation. At the heart of nurture is awareness of the confrontation. At the heart of discipline is concern for that corporate structure which allows forgiveness to become real. At the heart of shepherding is that concern which allows for confrontation and awareness in the individual. Pastoral theology speaks to and through each of these areas.

In the area of communication, pastoral theology is seen primarily in the offices of preaching and worship. This is not to say that these aspects of proclaiming and symbolizing forgiveness are not also involved in the other three areas. They are, however, dominant here.

For preaching, the concept of " realized forgiveness " means that the purpose of preaching is to interpret the Scripture so that the hearer can find what is being said to him through the Scripture. This reverses popular ideas as to success or failure in preaching. It is sometimes said, for example, that Paul failed in his sermon on Mars' Hill. Luke records that after that sermon, " some mocked; but others said, ' We will hear you again about this.' So Paul went out from among them. But some men joined him and believed " (Acts 17:32-34) . What really appears to have happened is that, through Paul, people found themselves free to react in three ways. Some became hostile and rejected what he had said, some decided that they would have to hear more, and some united with him. No one is reported to have been indifferent. If no one had heard anything, the sermon could well have been a failure. In view of the fact that everyone seems to have found the freedom to respond in one of the only three possible ways, the perspective that comes from " realized forgiveness " would rate this as highly successful.

For worship, the concept of " realized forgiveness " means that four parts must be reflected in the liturgy:

First, there must be the dimension of the context of forgiveness. This is usually accomplished through the form of a call to worship, an introit, a hymn of praise, or an invocation.

Second, within that context, there should then follow that which allows for awareness of the nature of one's sin and for the realization of the forgiveness of that sin. This is the negative aspect of confession. It is usually expressed in the confession and assurance of pardon. Kierkegaard has spoken of the need for silence so that one becomes aware of his need in the presence of God, not man. This gives opportunity for each person, in his own way, to express concretely the nature of his sin. The instrumentation of forgiveness is usually the assurance of pardon. In the light of what has been said about the dynamics of forgiveness, however, the worship service could well provide a means for expressing forgiveness of others. Forgiving others " as we would be forgiven " is one of the ways in which the reality of forgiveness has been most strongly expressed Biblically.

Third, the context of forgiveness is re-experienced at a deeper level as the freedom to hear the Scripture is made real. The Scripture and the sermon, then, become further avenues that both mediate the context of forgiveness and serve as instruments of making people aware of it.

Fourth, the instrumentation of this forgiveness is finally made real as an act of faith. This is the confession of faith. It may be expressed through a hymn, through the offering, through the expression of the Creed. The Sacrament itself is another level at which both the context and the instrument are found.

It is the task in communication constantly to seek the instrumentation that, indeed, does bring to one's awareness the context of forgiveness. This is not a subtle form of universalism that says any religion is as good as the Christian. Rather, it is to say that no one mediation and instrumentation of forgiveness in Christ is universal. The Spirit finds his expression everywhere, so that " each one heard them speaking in his own language " (Acts 2:6). It is the task of the area of communication to find that appropriate language which permits forgiveness to be realized as a fact in every situation.

For nurture, the concept of " realized forgiveness " relates primarily to experiencing the context and learning the symbols by which the context becomes real. This is generally associated with the office of teaching or education. Unfortunately, teaching is generally thought of strictly in terms of instrumentation. All the major denominations have revised their church school curricula in the past years. These revisions have been done with regard to the latest pedagogical insights. Information about personality development has been used to great advantage. As a result, many pastors have discovered that the students in their confirmation classes were theologically astute but personally dead. What had happened is that they had learned the new jargon as well as their grandparents had learned the jargon of the catechisms. This change, however, was merely a change in instrumentation.

"Realized forgiveness" means that education must be seen as a contextual function as well as an instrumental one. It means that no curriculum should begin without first having asked the question, "What will leave the student free to experience the truth that is to be presented — free to be personally alive?" It means that each curriculum will be concerned not just with facts but with helping the student learn the instrumentation by which the freedom to assimilate the facts can become real.

To see what this might mean operationally, the Westminster Presbyterian Church in Bloomfield, New Jersey, tried several approaches. First it sought to put educational publications into the hands of teachers. It found none available that related the contextual dimension to each theme or to any particular lesson. Although context may be a part of the basic philosophy, the church school materials are written primarily in terms of tools. Next, the church sought to solve the problem through lectures by pastors and elders. Even with group discussion, this did not meet the need.

Finally, the church has moved to the small-group experience. A group of twenty or thirty has gone away with the pastor for a twenty-four-hour period. The number was divided into smaller groups of ten. At the head of each was a layman who had a talent for facilitating rather than dominating discussion. A passage of Scripture was picked as a basis for discussion, but the conversation was permitted to move anywhere — and did. The pastor announced the agenda initially. Other than that, he was no more than a part of the discussion. There was also ample free time to be alone, talk with others, and relax.

The twenty-four-hour period ended with all groups coming together to share the insights of their discussions. The pastor then took time to reflect with the people on the nature of what had happened. This reflection in conversation was then brought to a focus and a close by a service of worship.

It would be optimistic to say that a majority discovered the church as a context in these groups. However, more than a few individuals did come to an awareness of the church as a context and not just as an instrument. Where this happened, then, the task was to help them find the ways in which what was real to them could become real to the classes they taught. These now understood education from the perspective of the experience of "realized forgiveness," and not just from the point of view of a tool.

In the area of college education, "realized forgiveness" means that a church-related college is such not because its students come from churches, or its charter is from a denomination, or it requires chapel and a certain number of courses in Bible. Rather, it means that a church-related college starts with the query, "What is the context and what is the instrumentation by which the freedom to hear the truth can become real to these students?" And in the area of seminary education, this perspective means that the student is not asked to be a part of a church-work program to gain technical competence. Rather, it means that the seminary community itself becomes a parish wherein a student can discover what it is to be free — i.e., to know the fullness of "realized forgiveness."

Pastoral theology, in the area of nurture, will also lead to questions about the pastoral office. It will lead to questions about whether or not the minister or teacher is to be seen as the father figure, the brother figure, or the mother figure that the sciences of man have proposed. It will do so, however, in a framework where these can come to be seen in a dynamic and meaningful relationship.

Pastoral theology in regard to discipline is usually thought of as the office of administration. As with education, the tendency here is to identify it with structure — with the instrumental dimension of forgiveness. The episcopal system tends to center upon the instrumental nature and forget about the contextual nature of the body of Christ. In so doing, it either forgets the other or degenerates into another form of sheer structure. In reaction to that, the congregational system tends to center on the contextual dimension. Presbyterianism seeks to be a system that is aware both of structure and context. Sadly, the result is often that one finds neither good context nor good instrumentation.

Although the area of discipline relates to the context and structure of a local parish, the place where it is having its most exciting development today is in the matter of church union. If the church is to be the body of Christ in which the context and instrumentation of " realized forgiveness " are maintained, then pastoral theology shows that these mergers cannot be just administrative. Although there will be structure, the lesson from pastoral theology is that the contextual aspect must be present first. There must be some means of experiencing the context of oneness in Christ or the administrative oneness will be hollow. This may be accomplished through some procedure of reordination that would recognize the validity of all clergy, vestrymen, and trustees across denominational lines — without organic union. This may be accomplished through a mutual recognition of the validity of the Sacrament of Communion across denominational lines. Whatever the formula, if the contextual as well as the administrative aspects are not seen, nothing genuine will happen.

The encouraging sign is that there seems to be growing awareness of the contextual nature of forgiveness in the area of discipline. For example, a European text on moral theology that is now being used in some American seminaries of the Roman Catholic Church begins:

The moral teaching of Jesus is contained in its totality in the glad tidings of salvation. The tremendous *Good News* is not actually a new law, but the Sovereign Majesty of God intervening in the person of Christ and the grace and love of God manifesting itself in Him. In consequence, all the precepts of the moral law, even the most sacred, are given a new and glorious orientation in divine grace and a new focus, the Person of the God-man.[27]

Although the book's development of moral theology is detailed and strange to Protestant ears, this predicating of it within the context of the person of Christ is familiar and important. The approach is a genuine change for many priests. (Similarities to the approach suggested by " realized forgiveness " are also evident in developments in the Eastern Orthodox Church.)

The shepherding perspective is so fully developed by Hiltner that hardly more can be added here. The concept of " realized forgiveness " would lead to an underscoring of the difference between pastoral care and psychotherapy. In practice, many ministers have confused the two. Psychotherapy is one of the healing arts, and there is an aspect of healing in pastoral care. Pastoral care, however, should be seen as that which allows the freedom to make use of the healing arts; it is not a substitute for them. A pastor may have all the training needed to be a therapist. Nevertheless, he needs to decide which he is going to be — a therapist or a pastor. In the pastoral analogy, a shepherd may have the training to be a veterinarian. However, if he is a good shepherd, when a sheep breaks a leg he had better send for a veterinarian to treat the sheep so that the work of shepherding the whole flock may continue. The two tasks are different.

IV Conclusion

The preceding two sections have been audacious. The more one reads in the areas of theology, the Bible, church history, and the " operational " fields, the more one is aware how much there is to learn and how great is the grasp of the scholars in their respective fields. Yet I have attempted to speak, because a word from the parish must be spoken. I may not have heard the Pelikans, the Barths, or the Hiltners in the way they wish to be heard. I do believe that I have heard the voice of the parish from which I speak.

In conclusion, then, I would say a word to the " angry young men " and to the uninformed who criticize the parish — particularly the suburban parish. There are two types of " angry young men." Some of these are men who speak out of their own weakness. The others are those who could succeed anywhere, but who have had the courage to answer the challenge of the mission field and the inner city. They speak not because they do not see but because they see too well the weaknesses of the parish. To these men, from the perspective of pastoral theology and " realized forgiveness," two comments are in order:

One, they should be careful lest they make the mistake of what Whitehead called " misplaced concreteness." The criticisms they make are right. Any sensitive parish minister could footnote them. Yet it is wrong to give up on the parish because of what is seen there. For criticisms of the noise of the solemn assemblies is a criticism of the instrumentation of forgiveness. To the " angry young man," it must be said: Your criticism is of just one aspect of the parish. Within the parish, every parish, there are those who stand with you in the body of Christ and who are seeking an instrumentation that genuinely allows for the realization of for- giveness. I grant that only ten percent of my parish may be aware of this " realized forgiveness "; and I would be happy if I thought that ten percent more were seeking it. Yet the point is that no area of society is free of the demonic. In the midst of his legiti- mate criticisms, I feel constrained to say from the parish that the " angry young man " sometimes seems more able to hear the questions that are coming from the Communists, from the Ten- nessee Williamses, and from the James Joyces, than from the man who, caught in a false peace, is earnestly asking help in finding true wholeness.

Two, not only is the parish not to be considered hopeless; *it is the great opportunity.* That statement is as true of the parish in suburbia as it is of the parish in the inner city. From the stand- point of pastoral theology, only within the church can the ones whom the " angry young men " criticize see their real problem. It is easy to speak of the captivity of the man in suburbia. Yet the fact that those men expose themselves to the body of Christ week after week is the great opportunity. Where that oppor- tunity is seen and the dynamics of forgiveness are understood, the fields are found white unto the harvest and the laborers few. The ten percent who understand have all that they can do.

Hence, when you who are today's prophets say, " Thus saith the Lord," — and we need you to say it — remember the remnant in Israel. For I submit that whenever " realized forgiveness " is translated into the language of the day, the parish is relevant; it is heard.

You ask, " Where? "

It was heard in the midst of a great national crisis by Martin Niemoeller. After his arrest, he said that when he was walking through the underground tunnel from the jail to the courthouse, he began to experience fear. He walked alone, and behind him walked the guard. In the hollowness of that tunnel, he heard a voice say: " The name of the Lord is a strong tower." The guard was the source of the voice. With it, Niemoeller experienced the context and the instrumentation of forgiveness. Records his biographer: " His fear had gone, and in its place was the calm brilliance of an utter trust in God." [28]

Again, the Word was heard in the midst of a deep personal crisis by a young widow in a church I served. Sixteen months after I had officiated at her marriage, her husband was killed in a helicopter crash. With her one-month-old child, she came to the church. To her friends, she seemed to be turning atheistic. Yet she attended services of worship, she came to the pastor in private, and she began to work with the youth group. She did become an atheist insofar as she found that the view of God she had had was false. Nevertheless, some nine months after her husband's burial, she knocked at my office door and said, " I stopped by for a moment just to tell you that I've found it; and it's real." She still had her nights of aloneness. She still had the pain that asked why an unfaithful neighbor lived when her husband died. She still had questions about faith. Her gain was awareness of a new oneness with God which gave her a basis for dealing with the aloneness, the pain, and the doubts. *It happened in the parish.*

The discipline of forgiveness is to give ourselves to others with such openness that they may hurt us. In fact, being human, they probably will hurt us despite themselves. Therefore, we must give of ourselves, forgiving in advance the trust they may betray. This does not mean to be stupid or, in a neurotic fashion, to become a Mr. Milquetoast. With parents, for example, giving of themselves may mean sacrificing popularity by denying a child something he wants. It does mean to recognize that when it comes to people, where there is no forgiveness, there is no life.

" Realized forgiveness " is the heart of the gospel. Why? Because the church knew in that first century, as it ought to know now, that when forgiveness is real, then the church is not only relevant, but through it God is heard.

Notes

CHAPTER 1

1. Paul Lehmann, *Forgiveness* (Harper & Brothers, 1940).
2. Eduard Thurneysen, *A Theology of Pastoral Care,* tr. by Jack A. Worthington and Thomas Wieser (John Knox Press, 1962), p. 182.
3. James G. Emerson, Jr., *Divorce, the Church, and Remarriage* (The Westminster Press, 1961), p. 23.
4. Martin E. Marty, *The Hidden Discipline* (Concordia Publishing House, 1962), p. xvii.
5. *Ibid.,* p. xvi.

CHAPTER 2

1. Arnold Toynbee, *A Study of History,* Vol. XII, *Reconsiderations* (Oxford University Press, 1961), p. 144.
2. Paul Tillich, *Systematic Theology* (The University of Chicago Press, 1951), Vol. I, p. 59.
3. Rudolf Bultmann, in *Kerygma and Myth,* tr. by Reginald Fuller, ed. by Hans Bartsch (S.P.C.K., London, 1953), p. 10.
4. *Ibid.*
5. Karl Barth, *Dogmatics in Outline,* tr. by C. Thompson (Harper Torchbooks, 1959), p. 11.
6. Reinhold Niebuhr, *The Self and the Drama of History* (Charles Scribner's Sons, 1955), p. 115.
7. *Ibid.,* p. 30.
8. L. Berkhof, *Systematic Theology* (Wm. B. Eerdmans Publishing Company, 1946), pp. 20–34.
9. Thurneysen, *op. cit.,* pp. 211 ff.
10. Seward Hiltner and Lowell Colston, *The Context of Pastoral Care* (Abingdon Press, 1961), p. 22.
11. *Ibid.,* pp. 29–30.
12. Carl R. Rogers and Rosalind F. Dymond, *Psychotherapy and Personality Change* (The University of Chicago Press, 1954). Used by permission.
13. Carl Rogers, *Client-Centered Therapy* (Houghton Mifflin Company, 1951), p. 513.

14. Rogers and Dymond, *op. cit.,* p. 13.
15. *Ibid.,* p. 77.
16. *Supra,* p. 31.
17. Hiltner and Colston, *op. cit.,* p. 197.
18. Rogers and Dymond, *op. cit.,* p. 79.
19. Added to the first shift-of-feeling sheet used.
20. Added to the second shift-of-feeling sheet used at a conference.

21. Summary definitions: (*a*) By " mediation," I mean that which stands between whatever is being expressed (love, forgiveness, hate) and the one to whom it is being expressed. (*b*) By " instrument," I mean strictly the tools by which something is accomplished. Sometimes the same thing may be both an instrument and a mediator at once. Consider a painting. To the observer, a painting mediates what was in the painter's mind. To the painter, the painting is the instrument that makes real what was in his mind. Similarly, my forgiving another is the way I make my own forgiveness real. At the same time, it mediates the context of my forgiveness to someone else. (*c*) By " dynamic," I mean the opposite of legalistic, rigid, or simple cause-effect views.

CHAPTER 3

1. The fundamentalist reviews, as opposed to the conservative ones, disturb me, for they seem totally oblivious to the fact that there is a methodological question in Bible study. They never come to grips with the part that personal subjectivity plays in their own approach to Scripture.

2. The fact that the Bible puts forgiveness at the center suggests that forgiveness is the central experience of the early church. In line with the typology set forth in Chapter 2, it could be said that this very experience of forgiveness gave the first church, and gives the church to-day, the freedom to create the canon.

3. For a discussion of the word " perspective " in pastoral theology, attention is called to the last chapter of this book and especially to the first chapters of Seward Hiltner's *Preface to Pastoral Theology.*

4. Each branch of theology has its key word which it both defines and needs. Without a Biblical theology, for example, we cannot be clear as to what we mean by revelation. Without a systematic theology, we do not get a doctrine of the Trinity. Likewise, without a pastoral theology, we do not come to an understanding of the meaning or proper us-age of the word " forgiveness."

The reverse is also true, for each of these words is crucial for the discipline in question. I recall an introductory lecture in urology at Billings Hospital, Chicago. The doctor held up a cystoscope and said, " Without this instrument, there is no urology." The science of urology discovers the instrument, and the instrument makes the science possible. So it is with each of these words. Without a doctrine of revelation, there could be no Biblical theology. Without a doctrine of the Trinity, there could be no Christian systematic theology. Pastoral theology has not yet identified the word that is the instrument it creates and without which it cannot exist as a theology. Presently, each definition of pastoral theology must identify that word or tool for itself until universal agreement is reached. For me, that tool is "realized forgiveness."

The Christian faith rises or falls on each key tool. Wherever one of them is lacking, that discipline as an expression of the Christian faith either dies or becomes irrelevant. In the early days of Biblical criticism, people panicked because they thought that analysis of the way in which the Bible was written meant no revelation. Throughout church history, an attack on the divinity or manhood of Christ has necessitated great apologies or defenders of the faith. In the present century, the need for a theology of the Holy Spirit is again required because, without it, the system of the faith becomes irrelevant.

In the Bible, when Paul wrote theologically, he seldom used the word "forgiveness." Yet, by contrast, the early church used it repeatedly. As I have already observed, by the act of selecting the Gospels, The Acts, and Revelation, the early church put forgiveness at the heart of the good news. Other non-Biblical documents, such as the Shepherd of Hermas, are preoccupied with the subject. Thus, the minute that the church found itself in a pastoral concern, the word "forgiveness" became central.

5. *The Interpreter's Dictionary of the Bible,* ed. by George A. Buttrick (Abingdon Press, 1962), Vol. II, p. 317.

6. Further, failure to see the distinction between forgiveness as a context and forgiveness as an instrument is found in all views that deny the reality of either free will or providence. From the standpoint of pastoral theology, the questions about the relation of free will and providence depend entirely upon the proper understanding of forgiveness. From the standpoint of forgiveness as a context, the emphasis must be on the reality of providence. There is no choice about the context. The context of God's forgiveness is present, regardless of human nature. From the standpoint of forgiveness as an instrument, the emphasis must be on the reality of free will. Each person is free to choose the instrument that works for him; indeed, each person must make that choice. A person is always free to reject the instrumentation of the context. Yet, within the total field of life's experience, neither providence nor free will can be denied.

7. James G. Emerson, Jr., *op. cit.,* pp. 34–44.

8. In the rigid or legalistic view, life is seen in a causal line fashion, which is very popular today because of the cause-effect theory in science. This theory, as it was developed by Newton and others, emphasizes the point that every effect must have a cause. For general purposes, this theory is helpful and effective. It was what pushed Freud to some of his

early insights. He wanted to find the cause of problems that did not seem to have a purely biological base. Yet, the concept of cause and effect has been substantially changed with the growth of atomic physics. "Cause and effect," as previously understood, was not precise enough for the work of research in magnetic fields. As a result, modern science has qualitatively changed the old views.

In religion, however, the old view still lingers. Life still is described by some persons as moving on a straight line. Life is pictured as having a beginning, A, an ending, Z, and events, B, D, and E, along the way. Biblically speaking, this cause-effect view is expressed in the legalistic interpretation of Scripture; but that method of Biblical interpretation is rejected by Scripture itself.

In the Old Testament, The Book of Job comes up again as a perfect example of that rejection. Job had more misfortune than a man can stand. He asked, "Why?" In subtle ways and blunt ways, his religious friends gave the answer: "You say that you have not sinned; yet, since these misfortunes have come upon you, you must have sinned." Job's friends were determined that every effect must have its cause. (The uncomfortable part of the story is that when we read the answers of Job's friends, we discover that they are the answers we would have given in the same situation. It is only after some reflection that we see what we really would be saying with those answers. It is only after some reflection that we recognize how much, in fact, we live our lives on the assumption of this rigid approach.) Thus, the whole book of Job stands as a rejection of the same view of cause and effect that modern science rejects.

In the New Testament, precisely the same is to be seen in the statements of Jesus. Based on the cause-effect idea, a great body of law had developed to determine what was work and what was not work, what was sin and what was not sin. Hence, when Jesus said, "You have heard that it was said to the men of old, 'You shall not kill.' But I say to you . . . ," he transformed the whole concept of law and sin. The simple, cause-effect view was no longer adequate.

The Biblical contradictions of this cause-effect method of interpretation are seen as clearly in the area of forgiveness as anywhere. In the sixth chapter of Matthew, Jesus commands that we forgive others if we are to be forgiven. On the cross, when he said, "Father, forgive them; for they know not what they do," Jesus asked forgiveness of people who were not forgiving. His command and his request are consistent only if forgiveness is seen as a field experience in which forgiving others is considered an instrument and Christ's forgiveness of others is understood as the context which makes that possible.

Further confirmation of the validity of the field approach in understanding the Biblical view of forgiveness is The First Letter of John.

There John says, "We love, because he first loved us." That text expresses, in one sentence, the contextual aspect of forgiveness.

9. In turning to the Scripture directly, we must first pay considerable attention to secondary sources. Those who disagree with these sources must remember that I am not writing a Biblical theology. Rather, I am asking of Biblical theology certain questions about the context and instrumentation of forgiveness. Future scholarship in the Biblical field will deepen, correct, and enlarge what is said here. As such, however, it will not alter the basic questions that pastoral theology asks of the Bible. Rather, changes in the research will give different answers to those questions.

10. William Gesenius, *Hebrew and Chaldee Lexicon,* tr. by S. P. Tregelles (Wm. B. Eerdmans Publishing Company, 1949), p. 588.

11. Robert B. Girdlestone, *Synonyms of the Old Testament* (Wm. B. Eerdmans Publishing Company, 1948 [reprint of 1897]), p. 135.

12. *Ibid.,* p. 136.

13. Gesenius, *op. cit.,* p. 463.

14. *Companion to the Bible,* ed. by J. J. von Allmen (Oxford University Press, Inc., 1958), p. 128.

15. To my knowledge, Oscar Cullmann, in *Christ and Time* (The Westminster Press, 1950), is the first one to develop this idea.

16. Rudolf Bultmann, *Theology of the New Testament* (Charles Scribner's Sons, 1957), Vol. I, p. 287.

17. Millar Burrows, *More Light on the Dead Sea Scrolls* (The Viking Press, Inc., 1958), p. 221.

18. At this point, forgiveness and atonement must not be confused. The two are related, but are not the same. The doctrine of the atonement has to do with the answer of systematic theology to the question of how the estrangement between God and man is overcome. Forgiveness has to do with the pastoral theological question of how man experiences freedom to be one with God. The death and resurrection of Christ gives this freedom because it is that which makes real the release of man from the demonic powers of the day.

19. Rudolf Bultmann, *op. cit.,* Vol. I, p. 36.

20. Millar Burrows, *The Dead Sea Scrolls* (The Viking Press, Inc., 1955), p. 189.

21. *Ibid.*

22. Gesenius, *op. cit.,* p. 374.

23. *The Interpreter's Dictionary of the Bible,* Vol. I, p. 725.

24. R. C. Trench, *Synonyms of the New Testament* (Wm. B. Eerdmans Publishing Company, 1948), p. 219.

25. It is interesting to note that Luke concludes his account with the instance of Jesus finally appearing to more of the disciples. In the context of that forgiveness, Jesus again " opened their minds to understand

the scriptures " (Luke 24:45) . Hence, we have a demonstration of the continuing interplay of the two poles within the overall field of forgiveness.

26. Marty, *op. cit.*, p. 2.
27. *Ibid.*, p. 32.
28. *Ibid.*, p. 65.
29. *Ibid.*, p. 68.
30. *Ibid.*, p. 70.
31. Girdlestone, *op. cit.*, p. 101.

CHAPTER 4

1. John T. McNeill, *Medieval Handbooks of Penance* (Columbia University Press, 1938) , p. 6. Quotations are used by permission.
2. *Ibid.*, p. 8.
3. *Ibid.*, p. 12.
4. *Ibid.*, p. 15.
5. John T. McNeill, *The Celtic Penitentials* (The University of Chicago Press, Doctor Dissertation, 1923) , p. 43.
6. Adolf von Harnack, *The Mission and Expansion of Christianity in the First Three Centuries,* tr. by James Moffatt (Harper Torchbooks, 1961) , p. 19.
7. W. R. Bowie, *Men of Fire* (Harper & Row, Publishers, Inc., 1962) , p. 36.
8. *The Apostolic Fathers,* tr. by F. Glimm, J. Marique, and G. Walsh (Vol. I of The Fathers of the Church) (Cima Publishing Company, Inc., 1947) , p. 200. Quotations are used by permission.
9. *Ibid.*, p. 175.
10. *Ibid.*, p. 73.
11. *Ibid.*, p. 218.
12. *Ibid.*, p. 238.
13. *Ibid.*, p. 263.
14. Williston Walker, *A History of the Christian Church* (T. & T. Clark, Edinburgh, 1932) , p. 160.
15. *The Confessions of Augustine,* tr. by J. G. Pilkington (Liveright Publishing Corporation, 1943) , p. 171.
16. *Ibid.*, p. 165.
17. *Ibid.*, p. 166.
18. *Ibid.*, p. 178.
19. *Ibid.*, p. 186.
20. From the standpoint of psychoanalysis, it makes no sense to raise questions about the emotional state of people like Augustine. Here, it might well be asked, " Did Augustine really have an experience of forgiveness? He emphasized that he no longer needed a wife, and that his mother found greater joy in his salvation than if he had given her grandchildren. Was Augustine's experience nothing more than giving

in to an Oedipus Complex? " Aside from the danger of trying to psychoanalyze a man at a distance of some seventeen hundred years, and aside from the fact that being forgiven does not mean that one is free from all one's neuroses, but rather is freer in one's ability to deal with them, the point is not relevant. Here, Augustine is being used as a clue to the way in which forgiveness was understood. Whether or not his own problems were solved, he does give us such a clue.

21. Pilkington, *op. cit.*, p. 175.

22. *Ibid.*, p. 177.

23. *The Writings of St. Augustine*, tr. by J. J. Gavigan and others (in The Fathers of the Church series) (Cima Publishing Company, Inc., 1947), Vol. IV, p. 246.

24. *Ibid.*, p. 460.

25. *Ibid.*, p. 440.

26. *Ibid.*

27. Augustine, *The City of God*, tr. by Marcus Dods (Modern Library, Inc., 1950), p. 692.

28. *The Writings of St. Augustine* (in The Fathers of the Church series), Vol. IV, p. 39.

29. *Ibid.*, p. 424.

30. *Ibid.*

31. *Ibid.*, p. 423.

32. *Ibid.*, p. 433.

33. *Ibid.*, p. 432.

34. *Ibid.*, p. 128.

35. *The Ante-Nicene Fathers*, ed. by A. Roberts and J. Donaldson (Wm. B. Eerdmans Publishing Company, 1950), Vol. II, p. 429. Quotations from this series are used by permission.

36. *Ibid.*, p. 216.

37. *Ibid.*

38. *Ibid.*, p. 217.

39. *Ibid.*, p. 219.

40. *Ibid.*, p. 220.

41. *Ibid.*, p. 230.

42. *The Ante-Nicene Fathers*, Vol. IV, p. 239.

43. Robert Payne, *The Holy Fire* (Harper & Brothers, 1957), p. 235.

44. James Hastings, *Encyclopedia of Religion and Ethics* (Charles Scribner's Sons, 1910), Vol. II, p. 170.

45. *The Ante-Nicene Fathers*, Vol. IV, p. xxix.

46. *Ibid.*, p. 60, sec. 44.

47. *Ibid.*, p. 61, sec. 45.

48. Jaroslav Pelikan, *The Light of the World* (Harper & Row, Publishers, Inc., 1962), pp. 75–76.

49. *The Nicene and Post-Nicene Fathers*, ed. by A. Roberts (Wm. B. Eerdmans Publishing Company, 1956), Vol. IV, para. 47, p. 29.

50. *Ibid.,* para. 49, p. 335.

51. *Ibid.,* para. 10, p. 41.

52. *Ibid.,* " Life of Antony," para. 4, p. 196.

53. *Ibid.,* para. 21, p. 202.

54. *Ibid.,* para. 22, p. 202.

55. *Ibid.,* para. 45, p. 208.

56. *Ibid.,* para. 19, p. 201.

57. *Ibid.,* " Letter VII for Easter," A.D. 335, p. 527.

58. *The Apostolic Fathers* (Vol. I of The Fathers of the Church), p. 74.

59. *The Writings of St. Augustine* (in The Fathers of the Church series), Vol. IV, p. 425.

60. Harnack, *op. cit.,* p. 98.

61. *The Apostolic Fathers* (Vol. I of The Fathers of the Church), p. 218.

62. *Ibid.,* p. 214.

63. *Ibid.,* p. 42.

64. *Ibid.,* p. 74.

65. Payne, *op. cit.,* p. 139.

66. *The Ante-Nicene Fathers,* Vol. III, article on repentance.

CHAPTER 5

1. Emerson, *op. cit.,* p. 96.

2. *The Journal of George Fox,* a rev. ed. by John L. Nickalls (Cambridge University Press, 1952), p. 17.

3. *Ibid.*

4. John T. McNeill, *A History of the Cure of Souls* (Harper & Brothers, 1951), p. 112.

5. *Ibid.,* p. 113.

6. McNeill, *Medieval Handbooks of Penance,* p. 251.

7. *Ibid.*

8. *Ibid.,* p. 195.

9. McNeill, *A History of the Cure of Souls,* p. 123.

10. McNeill, *Medieval Handbooks of Penance,* p. 142.

11. *Ibid.,* p. 300.

12. *Ibid.,* p. 302.

13. *Ibid.,* pp. 300–301.

14. McNeill, *A History of the Cure of Souls,* p. 163.

15. John Calvin, *Institutes of the Christian Religion,* ed. by John T. McNeill, tr. by Ford Lewis Battles (The Westminster Press, The Library of Christian Classics, Vols. XX–XXI, 1960), III. iii. 24.

16. At this point, some may raise the question as to whether or not everyone is given this grace. The question of providence and predestination is not an issue here, for that is a question of systematic theology rather than pastoral. The point of pastoral theology would be that it is

only from the perspective of forgiveness that the question of free will, foreknowledge, and predestination makes sense. The trouble with many interpretations of this point is that most people begin with Calvin's Christology and move to his view of the church and forgiveness. Actually, one should start with Calvin's view of the corporate aspect of life and the place of forgiveness. No one has, as yet, done a full statement of freedom in Calvin from the point of view of forgiveness. My own thinking on the place to begin is expressed more fully in *Divorce, the Church, and Remarriage*. The place of his corporate view is expressed in the writings of Thurneysen, Barth, and McNeill.

17. Calvin, *Institutes,* III. xx. 9.

18. *Ibid.,* III. xx. 17.

19. William Telfer, *Forgiveness of Sins* (SCM Press, Ltd., London, 1959) , p. 109.

20. *A Compendium of Luther's Theology,* ed. by Hugh Thomson Kerr, Jr. (The Westminster Press, 1943) , p. 87.

21. Telfer, *op. cit.,* p. 112.

22. *A Compendium of Luther's Theology,* p. 86.

23. Telfer, *op. cit.,* p. 116.

24. *A Compendium of Luther's Theology,* p. 86.

25. Calvin, *Institutes,* IV. i. 21.

26. *Ibid.,* IV. i. 4.

27. Emerson, *op. cit.,* pp. 104–105.

28. Calvin, *Institutes,* IV. i. 22.

29. *Ibid.,* III. iii. 19.

30. *Ibid.,* III. xx. 45.

31. *Ibid.,* III. xx. 9.

32. *Ibid.*

33. *Ibid.,* III. xi. 21.

34. *Ibid.*

35. *Luther: Early Theological Works,* ed. and tr. by James Atkinson (The Westminster Press, The Library of Christian Classics, Vol. XVI, 1962) , p. 33.

36. *Ibid.,* p. 70.

37. *Ibid.,* p. 271.

38. *Ibid.,* p. 276.

39. *Ibid.,* p. 74.

40. *Works of Martin Luther,* organized by Adolph Spaeth (A. J. Holman Company, 1916) , p. 354.

41. Telfer, *op. cit.,* p. 117.

42. *Sacraments and Forgiveness,* ed. by Paul F. Palmer (Vol. II in Sources of Christian Theology) (The Newman Press, 1960) , pp. 249–250.

43. John Bunyan, *Grace Abounding to the Chief of Sinners* (Bradley Garretson & Company, 1872) , p. 29.

44. *Ibid.,* p. 30.
45. *Ibid.,* p. 32.
46. *Ibid.,* p. 46.
47. *Ibid.,* p. 57.
48. *Ibid.,* p. 56.
49. John Bunyan, *Account of the Author's Call to the Ministry* (Bradley Garretson & Company, 1872) , p. 64.
50. Jonathan Edwards, *Religious Affections,* ed. by John E. Smith (Yale University Press, 1959) , p. 17.
51. F. Schleiermacher, *The Christian Faith,* tr. by J. R. Mackintosh and J. S. Stewart (T. & T. Clark, Edinburgh, 1928) , p. 6.
52. *Ibid.,* p. 16.
53. *Ibid.,* p. 126.
54. *Ibid.,* p. 361.
55. A. Ritschl, *The Christian Doctrine of Justification and Reconciliation,* tr. by H. R. Mackintosh and A. B. Macaulay (Charles Scribner's Sons, 1900) , p. 1.
56. *Ibid.,* p. 56.
57. *Ibid.,* p. 108.
58. *Ibid.,* p. 391.
59. Walter Rauschenbusch, *Christianizing the Social Order* (The Macmillan Company, 1912) , p. 1.
60. Walter Rauschenbusch, *A Gospel for the Social Awakening,* ed. by Benjamin Mays (Association Press, 1950) , p. 32.
61. *Ibid.,* p. 46.
62. Walter Rauschenbusch, *Christianity and Social Crisis* (The Macmillan Company, 1907) , p. 57.
63. Rauschenbusch, *A Gospel for the Social Awakening,* p. 47.
64. *Ibid.,* p. 110.
65. *Ibid.,* p. 149.

CHAPTER 6

1. These are not questions out of the human intellect, but out of the human soul. The answer cannot be out of abstract theology, but only out of the Holy Spirit. Henry Pitney Van Dusen makes the point well when, in discussing the doctrine of God, he suggests that we should speak of " Spirit, Son, Father," rather than " Father, Son, and Holy Spirit." Van Dusen might even hold that what I have described as the essence of pastoral theology is really the doctrine of the Holy Spirit. If one wishes to say that the doctrine of the Holy Spirit can be discussed from both the point of view of the parish and the point of view of systematics, that may be true. The point to be grasped is that we all start where we are and with the impact that the Spirit has made on us. The Christian may proclaim Jesus Christ as the answer, but it is the Holy Spirit that came first. It is the Holy Spirit that both makes the

proclamation possible and allows it to be heard.

2. How one solves this separation by his understanding of forgiveness depends upon one's view of personality. The late A. J. Carlson, of Chicago, often expressed his thoughts on the lecture platform. "Your personality is nothing but a matter of complex neurological organization," he would say. If personality is seen as no more than a force, like gravity, then wholeness will be understood in relation to some form of unified field theory that holds the universe together. In that case, realization of forgiveness becomes nothing more than a part of sub-atomic physics.

If, however, personality is seen as something that is qualitatively different from sheer force — no matter how close the analogy — then, ultimately, we come to the word "God." By analogy, just as there is a field of gravity in which all physical elements move and live and have their being, so also is there a field of personality. In relation to this view, the question is: "What allows for integrity, oneness, wholeness, and the end of separation between me and that in which all life holds together and has meaning? "

It is in answer to that question that we could say before, " the *mediation* is Jesus Christ."

3. Bard Thompson, *Liturgies of the Western Church* (The World Publishing Company, 1961) .

4. *Ibid.,* p. 8.

5. *Ibid.,* p. 48.

6. *Ibid.,* p. 161.

7. *Ibid.*

8. Karl Barth, *God in Action,* tr. by E. G. Homrighausen and K. J. Ernst (Round Table Press, 1936, reprint 1963) , p. 66.

9. Karl Barth, *Evangelical Theology: An Introduction* (Holt, Rinehart, and Winston, Inc., 1963) , p. 18.

10. *Ibid.,* p. 55.

11. *Ibid.,* p. 56.

12. *Ibid.,* pp. 90–91.

13. Thurneysen, *op. cit.,* p. 207.

14. Barth, *God in Action,* p. 55.

15. Tillich, *Systematic Theology,* Vol. I, p. 32.

16. *Ibid.,* p. 33.

17. *Ibid.,* p. 62.

18. Paul Tillich, *The Courage to Be* (Yale University Press, 1952) , p. 164.

19. *Ibid.,* p. 165.

20. Matthew Spinka entitles a book on the thought of Berdyaev in this manner.

21. N. Berdyaev, *The Beginning and the End* (Harper & Row, Publishers, Inc., 1957, paperback) , p. vii.

22. *Ibid.*, p. 248.

23. *Ibid.*, pp. 104 ff.

24. Reinhold Niebuhr, " The Tyranny of Science," in *The Thought of Reinhold Niebuhr*, by Gordon Harland (Oxford University Press, Inc., 1960) , p. 68.

25. Seward Hiltner, *Preface to Pastoral Theology* (Abingdon Press, 1958) , p. 15.

26. *Ibid.*, p. 28.

27. Bernhard Häring, *The Law of Christ*, tr. by Edwin G. Kaiser (Vol. I in General Moral Theology) (The Newman Press, 1963) , p. 2.

28. Dietmar Schmidt, *Pastor Niemöller*, tr. by Lawrence Wilson (Doubleday & Company, Inc., 1959) .

Index